M000238847

RADICAL HOPE AND THE HEALING POWER OF ILLNESS

Daphne Publications

Radical Hope and the Healing Power of Illness

A Jungian Guide to Exploring the Body, Mind, Spirit Connection to Healing

BUD HARRIS, PH.D.

DAPHNE PUBLICATIONS • ASHEVILLE, NORTH CAROLINA

DAPHNE PUBLICATIONS, AN IMPRINT OF SPES, INC.

Harris, Clifton T. Bud
Radical hope and the healing power of illness: a Jungian guide to exploring the body, mind, spirit connection to healing / Bud Harris

ISBN 978-0-692-77639-1   Non-Fiction
1. Body, Mind, Spirit 2. Healing 3. Spirituality 4. Jungian Psychology

Cover Design: Courtney Tiberio
Cover Photography: blueeyes/Shutterstock
Interior Design: Susan L. Yost
Illustrations: Dana Irwin

To my daughter, Marjorie

CONTENTS

Acknowledgments

Like all of my books, this book is a product of my years of experiences and reflections. A special thanks is due to the men, women, and children whom I've been privileged to know and work with in my professional life. I want to assure all of them—who have labored to heal, to understand themselves, and to grow through life's challenges—that the stories in this book are fictionalized compositions. They have evolved from my thirty-five-plus years of experience and are typical of real-life situations without being based on the actual experiences of a particular person. The quotations that begin each chapter all come from the lovely book of poems and essays, *To Bless the Space Between Us* by John O'Donohue.

My wife, Massimilla Harris, Ph.D., Gail Rogers, M.A., and Marnie Muller, M.L.A. have graciously supported my writing, generously affirmed it, challenged me to improve it, and helped me stretch beyond my limits in almost every sentence I wrote. I am blessed to have such help in my corner.

PREFACE

"I really did, and do believe that my life is perfect, although I recognize that certain details of it—like my own advancing debilitation by multiple sclerosis and my husband's metastic melanoma—might seem from the outside world to forbid it such status…

"The outside," however, never provides a good vantage point for life study… The truth is also that "perfect" may mean "flawless." It may mean "consummate" or "whole" as well, and it is in this sense that I cherish my life as I could not, perhaps, without its flaws. That is, these force me to live daily at the potential end of the world as I know it. And so, on any given day, my life must be as fully made as I can make it: perfect."

– NANCY MAIRS
VOICE LESSONS

This book is written for you…

If you are suffering from a chronic or critical illness or an auto-immune disease…It is also written for you if you have a loved one suffering from an illness…or if you are a caregiver or professional who helps people. This book is especially written for you if you are seeking to understand the meaning of illness in our lives and how it can lead us to a new sense of wholeness and of who we are…and into the depth of what it means to be fully human. It also explores how, in our journey to become whole and fully human, we can encounter the nature of the Divine within ourselves.

For over thirty-five years, I have practiced as a psychotherapist, psychologist, and Zurich-trained Jungian psychoanalyst. I have lectured and given workshops around the country and have corresponded with readers of my numerous books for over twenty-five years. During these years, I have worked with people with a host of various illnesses and with others who were facing the end of their lives. I have also worked with those with emotional and psychological challenges, as well as with people who simply wanted to have a more fulfilling life. Many of these people have been intensely interested in finding out the meaning of their experience, or finding out if it has meaning. They have also wanted to find out what the meaning of healing and wholeness can be…and how that may or may not relate to a cure.

Of course, I approach my work from the Jungian perspective as it is realized in my professional and personal experiences. In my own life and in case after case in my practice, as well as in my professional field, I have seen how important it is to understand how to create a healing and growthful environment within ourselves, and how doing this can revitalize our entire life. I have spent decades in formal studies and have used this formal knowledge and professional training to help me learn from my own struggles, suffering, and journey of individuation. I find that if we truly face ourselves and life, we will naturally inspire, encourage, comfort, and help each other. This book, *Radical Hope*, is designed to help us reengage with the deepest parts of ourselves in order to release the power of radical hope in our lives and to return home to ourselves. This is an approach that empowers us to live more intensely, with more vitality and love. In this book, I want to share what I have learned with you and do all that I can to revitalize the true meaning of healing in our lives. My intention is to help you create an environment that fosters healing and wholeness within yourself so that you can take this journey…of finding healing from your grief and relief from your fears.

Illness burns away the patterns of living and being that have been imposed upon us by circumstances and our histories with other people. Illness changes the fundamental assumptions that have given our lives their particular meanings and leaves us in a state that doesn't immediately make sense. But we are still left with life's questions: What is the purpose of my life? Why am I here? Do my sufferings and struggles have meaning? What am I doing?

The compelling questions for me are: How can I help you? How can I share with you what I have learned? How can I share the depth of life and glory that rises like a phoenix out of the ashes, out of the horror and the beauty that being fully engaged in life brings? And why should you even listen to me? My answer is to ask you to consider listening to what I am saying if it touches your heart…to pay attention if it touches your soul…and to work through these pages as you search for radical hope. Read on…even if you begin this work reading through desperate and bitter tears.

The promise I was looking for many years ago was the love of life, and through this inner journey, I have found it. I hope that you do as well. If I look back over my life, it looks like a tragedy from the standpoint of illness. My sister had cancer at age two and a half, and my mother died of it when I was fourteen. My first wife began a tragic and heartbreaking slide into schizophrenia in her late twenties. My father, too, died from a long struggle with cancer. Now my daughter is struggling with multiple sclerosis, and I have experienced my own cancer. In my practice, I have worked with people with many illnesses, from AIDS to chronic fatigue syndrome. Yes, it has all been very hard, but "hard" doesn't mean bad or tragic. Look at me and judge that for yourself. Now I want to share the path to the depths and glory of life's possibilities that can arise anew from the ashes of our experiences.

Illness forces us to pay attention to ourselves. When we wake up to the call in our illnesses, we learn to treat ourselves and our lives as sacred. The journey through this book and its exercises will help you learn to treat yourself and your life as sacred. The exercises are quietly powerful. They bring clarity, hope, and a new relationship to yourself and to life. They are designed to stimulate, inspire, and comfort you while being a road map for the journey into radical hope. On some days they will challenge you. On other days they may help you experience the flow of love and creativity that supports life. There also may be days when life is turbulent…and these exercises can become an anchor, helping you hold fast against the wind.

Far too many of us spend years struggling and suffering after finding out about our diagnoses and then living in secret dread before we discover we have to rebirth ourselves…and that we have to be willing to face the mental and emotional work in order for this rebirth to happen. Sadly, far too many people never discover this turning point. This book is meant to help us turn this corner toward radical hope by helping us build our consciousness and self-awareness step by step and by assisting us to uncover our inner strength and deepen our engagement in life.

This process has to begin with figuring out how to know ourselves. In really learning to know ourselves, we develop our ability to be compassionate with ourselves. We discover how to "suffer with" ourselves and also realize how to honor our past instead of despising it or having naïve illusions about it. This approach is also true for our illnesses…we learn how to have compassion for ourselves and how to honor our illness, though that doesn't mean we have to embrace it or like it. And we come to understand that, paradoxically, any compassion we offer to others that isn't truly grounded in our own self-compassion is shallow, hypocritical, and a pretense. As we change our own lives, we help change the heart of our culture by acknowledging this reality, and in doing so, we help others get started sooner in this understanding.

Make no mistake…life and my greater Self thrust me into this transforming, surprising journey. Leaving my business and going back to school to become a psychologist and then a Jungian analyst "appeared on the surface" as a journey of self-actualization. However, this description—"a journey of self-actualization"—was the persona of my journey. I supported this image and I hid behind it. But beneath the surface, it was my first wife's schizophrenia—the surprise, the terror, and the helplessness of it—that took me on a search into trying to understand her suffering as well as that of our three children and myself. This search led me into the heart of depth psychology, the Jungian approach, and ultimately into myself.

Since my daughter's diagnosis of multiple sclerosis in 2004, I have been strongly motivated to focus a great deal of my studying and work on psychology and illness. Every illness has a psychological component. Every illness affects our emotions and our feelings of safety, identity, and trust in life. This doesn't mean that an illness is caused "psychologically" or that it can be cured psychologically. Our personal psychology, though, often participates in the cause of an illness or our particular vulnerability to one. Yet through the inner journey of individuation into healing and wholeness, we can do a great deal to create a healing environment within ourselves and our life. By following this path, we can give maximum support to our possibilities for a cure and for living an enriched life with humor, vitality, and purpose.

Illness brings us face to face with the death process. This includes the death of our old selves as well as the recognition of the hollowness of our culture's ideas of success and the good life. It can also mean the death of our expectations for the future and the death of our notions of control. In addition, illness often brings feelings of humiliation, helplessness, and dependency while destroying for us many of our society's shallow ideas about love. I hope that my words and the steps in this book will guide you into the best way to handle these events by seeing them differently.

Illness can be regarded as a call...as part of creation's cycle of transformation...calling us to a whole new life, a new self. It can also be seen as a call to become more fully human, more deeply engaged in life. It is a way to learn more profoundly that life is joy and sorrow...horror and beauty. This book guides you through the process of learning how to encounter more directly and more keenly the depths of the feelings that connect you to life, and it also helps you to understand how to not let these feelings define you. This process describes how your suffering could turn into a "birth canal" for a new life. Yet it also emphasizes how important it is to honor the suffering itself, because it isn't simply a passage—it is real, and you have a right to take time and space to weep, cry, rage, and despair. Even psychic deaths need to be mourned, as we shall see, because they are the loss of things that were important to us.

Loving life requires accepting loss. It is unfortunate that our culture—especially through media commercials, as well as through "positive thinking," religious, and pop-psych approaches—teaches us that loss and hardship are bad. In actuality, our losses, our illnesses, and our hardships may have a deeper meaning and may be able to transform those of us who can accept the fullness of our humanity when touched by their searing grace. Such transformations, though, require devotion and effort. Yet sometimes they yield what some folks consider miracles.

But it is naïve to believe that spiritual growth, awareness, or consciousness will somehow remove the experiences or trials that we humans have to face.

The path of psychological and spiritual growth as outlined here does not change life. It changes our relationship to life…our engagement in life, and it changes how we approach and experience our suffering. When we quit denying illness, accept that it is actually quite common—more common than vibrant health—we then quit making ourselves and others who are ill feel like outcasts. An important part of this journey is to value the people who are ill in our midst (many of whom appear normal), to recognize them, to care for them, and also to honor ourselves.

This book is written to be your personal guide to help you learn more about:

1. The emotional impact of an illness on our personality

2. The emotional impact of an illness on our loved ones and our caregivers

3. How the goal of Jungian psychology is to grow through our problems and illnesses to a place beyond "normal"

4. How to awaken from the spell of "the good life" and the trance of "conventional, normal wisdom" that keep us trapped and limit our healing potentials

5. The steps to take in "a journey to a place beyond normal" and how to embark on this journey

6. How our illness and struggles can fuel our transformation to empower, enlarge, and deepen us

7. How to cultivate our imagination so it can become a path to inner healing, authentic living, and growth…and form our relationship to our greater Self, the source of our vitality, inner unity, and peace

8. The questions to ask our shadow, dream figures, symptoms, and illnesses as we proceed on this journey

9. How to tap the creative responses from our unconscious and the potentials in our "unlived" lives and how journaling, active imagination, and rituals can become pathways for communicating with our unconscious and the Self

10. How our inner work may aid our medical treatments

11. How, through our inner work and our greater Self, we learn how to experience the unity of our minds, bodies, and Spirit

12. How our experiences of illness and death are meant to teach us, on a very personal level, that life is sacred and precious

As I have said, illness compels us to devote our attention to ourselves, and when we wake up to the call in our illnesses, we come to learn to treat ourselves and our lives as sacred. If we cannot do that for ourselves, we cannot really treat others and their lives as sacred either.

The purpose of this book and its exercises is to assist in this journey to wake up and devote attention to ourselves...to learn to treat ourselves and our lives as sacred. Let me say again that these exercises are quietly powerful. They bring clarity, hope, and a new relationship to ourselves and to life. They are designed to stimulate, inspire, and comfort you while being a road map for the journey into radical hope.

This book is filled with reflections and exercises designed to help you on this path. A life that is being lived fully is creative, loving, and difficult. I doubt that I can convey to you the feeling of the miraculous that you can learn to experience. Yet I am inviting you to join me to find out for yourself what it means to let your illness teach you how to live a life beyond normal.

– BUD HARRIS, PH.D.
ASHEVILLE, NC

At the end of each chapter, you will have the opportunity to go deep within and reflect upon questions that may stir strong feelings inside you…Use them as guideposts to listen to yourself.

I would like to invite you to journal your thoughts and your feelings—to write, to draw, to even scribble…and take your time. This is important work. Feel free to change your mind, to add more at a later time, and to expand to a larger personal journal. Be creative and take risks. Look deep within as you meet and discover your authentic self.

Remember, you are not trying to "fix" yourself. You are learning how to treasure who you really are…and your life. Even though this journey may begin with the shock of an illness diagnosis, it is allowing you to go deeper, perhaps more than you have ever imagined.

INTRODUCTION

In the beginning
The Word was red,
And the sound was thunder,
And the wound in the unseen
Spilled forth the red weather of being.

— John O'Donohue

As my life entered its second half, I renewed a childhood interest... and became enchanted again with the stories in myths and fairy tales. One of these was the myth of the phoenix. Growing up in Atlanta, Georgia, a city that had burned to the ground in the War Between the States and then rebuilt and adopted the phoenix as its symbol, this image was implanted in my mind at an early age. In these mythic stories, the phoenix, or the firebird, is a remarkable creature with a lot to teach us if we can enter the world of imagination and human destiny—the archetypal world.

In fairy tales, this elegant bird has majestic plumage, with feathers that glow like a bonfire. One feather can light an entire room. Typically in these stories, the phoenix represents a difficult quest. The quest usually begins when the hero finds a lost tail feather and sets out to capture the live bird. Frequently the quest is to save a kingdom, to please a king, or to win a bride. But in classic fairy-tale style, the feather is a premonition of the start of a hard journey, with magical helpers along the way who assist the hero or heroine. The ingredients of the classic fairy tale are all here, where something is lacking in the kingdom, or in the life of the king, or in the life of the hero or heroine. Then a marvel is glimpsed, and an arduous journey begins. Help is discovered by the hero or heroine, who undertakes the journey with courage and humility. The journey is to faraway lands, and the return brings new life and transformation to the whole story.

The myth of the phoenix, though, brings an entirely new dimension to the story of the firebird. The phoenix, the beautiful bird with elegant plumage, has a journey all its own, a solitary journey. At the end of a particular cycle in its life, it builds an exquisite and fragrant nest. Then this beautiful bird ignites the nest and is consumed in its own flames. This bird symbolizes part of the journey of our own lives. It shows us that the fire of life, the fire of being fully alive, of being fully engaged in life, is both beautiful and gives birth to us, and also destroys us. Old selves, no matter how good, will be destroyed in order to be reborn in the transformational processes of a life being lived. Seeing these two patterns—the arduous journey initiated by a bright glimmer of hope, as well as the necessity to participate in our own death and rebirth—introduces us to the patterns and wisdom underlying our lives. That is how I came to pick the phoenix for the symbol of my work with illness.

◆ ◆ ◆

In spite of my many years of training and experience, I still felt helpless in trying to assist my daughter in dealing with her progressive multiple sclerosis that was diagnosed in 2004. I felt helpless in my efforts to help her find healing, to find meaning in her experiences, to find more wholeness, to touch something deep within herself that would bring the inner hidden hands to support her, and to help her know that this inner presence cares about her and loves her. I have watched her struggle, hope for cures, and hope for medications that might slow the process of the disease. As she lost control of her body, as she fought to keep her spirit, wrestled with hopelessness, and strove to love her family…I felt powerless. And as her lack of control increased, I felt even more powerless. So I tried to listen, and I prayed.

While the days were passing, I often found myself awake in the early morning hours, driven out of sleep by thinking about her pain or my own. Sometimes I wondered what difference it makes to seek, to search, and to follow the pattern of my destiny…which is to be a seeker and a searcher. Yet even when I was finally drifting back into sleep, I could still hear a small voice coming from the depths of my heart saying, "It makes a difference—don't stop." I also spent a lot of time searching for ways that my psychology could help her—if not her, and maybe not even me, then at least others who can benefit from our journey.

I am on the quest once again to find a way to alleviate soul-pain—in this case, our soul-pain and that of our families. In the past, I have found inner support rising from the ground of my being that could bring a relief to pain and especially to the fear and anxiety that is clutching at us. And this same support, when we find it, helps us admit to ourselves that our old selves are dead, our old ways of life are dead, and that we must be willing to let so many of our old ideals, values, obligations, and things we loved about life and ourselves die too.

While I reflect on these thoughts, some of my favorite lines that I have pondered for years from T. S. Eliot's poem "East Coker" come to mind and soothe my soul. His words bring both comfort and direction as he writes:

I said to my soul, be still, and wait without hope
For hope would be hope for the wrong thing; wait without love
For love would be love of the wrong thing; there is yet faith
But the faith and the love and the hope are all in the waiting.
Wait without thought, for you are not ready for thought;
So the darkness shall be the light, and the stillness the dancing.

The dancing is not to dance as if nothing happened. It is to acknowledge that something drastic has happened, the collapse of an old way of life or an old self, and then…to dance. It is an approach to life that reminds me that even while we are on this bitter path, we can become receptive in our helplessness to something new, something beyond our imagination, being born. This path is so scary, yet it is the best way we can continue to be cocreators of life with the Divine through the deep Self within us that holds us. It is the dance that Zorba did at the end of his story—the dance that celebrates life after facing disaster. This is the dance that is a radical acceptance of life.

◆ ◆ ◆

As I continued my series of reflections on an icy winter's day about my daughter and her illness, the meaning of the winter solstice lingered in my mind. Weeks ago, night had reached its zenith, and daylight began to increase. Will that happen in our lives too? I asked. Have we reached that point? How do we reach that turning point? Surely it is archetypal, an eternal symbol of promise in the universe. Our fear of the dark is also archetypal—especially the fear of an unknown amount of suffering that may lie in front of us and the loss of a familiar, predictable world that will support a vision of a happy future. These fears, when dramatically activated, become the genesis of what I am calling "soul-pain." This is the searing, deep pain that makes us feel like we have lost ourselves or much that is dearest to us and that scares us into turning against ourselves—that causes us to cut ourselves off from the support of our inner depths and to see our inner lives as threatening rather than supporting.

In his remarkable set of journals titled the *Red Book*, Jung says, "When I comprehended my darkness, a truly magnificent night came over me and my dream plunged me into the depth of the millennia and from it my phoenix ascended" (p. 274). In my journey into the darkness that I've described, the darkness exerted a terrible disciplining on the tyranny of my expectations and especially on my longing to have power and control over the nature of what I can do. But of course this darkness is only a beginning. And the archetypal process of transformation turns bitter and destructive if we try to sit numbly or dumbly through it. Without my full engagement, just as Jacob wrestled for his life with the angel in the night, the archetypal journey toward the light, toward renewal, doesn't begin. I must experience the darkness and awaken to it consciously. I must seek to deepen it and my consciousness of it. And I must make radical sacrifices that fulfill the religious meanings of the word sacrifice, which is to make sacred and help us come closer to the Divine. Only my truest tears can be transformed into pearls, and it is only from the fire and ashes of my life that a phoenix can emerge anew. The same is true for my daughter and our loved ones. To be reborn, the phoenix must be consumed in its nest of flames. Psychologically, this image tells me that in the face of a shattering illness, we must accept the reality of the radical sacrifices required of us in order to face life…standing on our own two feet and demanding meaning from it.

Slowly, over decades of confronting myself and life…and through the veil of tormented tears, I have learned that I must sacrifice my greatest fear. That fear is the fear that if I accept my reality completely, I will be overpowered or defeated by it or by despair and hopelessness.

Again and again, in one new circumstance after another, I have been forced to learn and relearn that accepting the reality of my experiences is the only real way that I can find enough separation from them to be able to assume an attitude toward them.

Paradoxically, this acceptance and separation allows me to have compassion with myself—to "suffer with" myself. Through the sacrifice of my fear, I can pass through a doorway that leads to receptivity—that beautiful aspect of the archetypal feminine within me. As I become more receptive to my reality, I find another door that then opens to the wellspring of life within me. Through this doorway, I pass into a fiercer suffering that is linked to the whole of life, and then, instead of being crushed, the pain, though piercing, becomes lighter. It is at this point that I reach the possibility of becoming a vessel through which new life can emerge, even if I am sick and dying.

I must sacrifice another fear as well, and so must my daughter. This is the fear of giving up my normal, systematic way of thinking, viewing, and evaluating myself. And along with this, I must sacrifice the illusion that there is, or ever was, the possibility of a calm and happy life that works smoothly if we can figure out how to do it or how "to get it right." Our traditional view is to fight the darkness, not to accept it. We try to cheer ourselves up, to have happy pleasant thoughts, and to put on a positive attitude in order to try to overcome the darkness and return to "normal." We exhaust ourselves trying to marshal the heroic power to overcome our darkness and defeat it without realizing we are fighting ourselves and may be holding back the dark side of the transformative reality we need to face, and that our efforts are aborting our own rebirth. Tears of grief and tears of rage can be the stuff of future pearls, for they can be great expressions of being alive. Denial, repression, and shirking such pain lead to the deadness of depression, a surrender to helplessness, and frequently a deeper collapse into fear. Rage can be a rage against the pull to give up and slowly slip beneath the waves of life into a living death where we can no longer initiate anything.

Accepting the darkness is a **radical** change in our perspective, and **deepening** it is even more radical. But these radical changes in our perspective release us so we can value accepting the dark and experiencing the full reality of our fear, pain, and loss. And those experiences allow the other radical archetypal change to begin and proceed toward the birth of new light from the well of darkness. For my daughter, or for any of us, acceptance doesn't mean giving up treatment, or surrendering to or embracing her illness.

To long for life is to get the very best of medical care and to do everything we can to enhance the healing environments around and within ourselves. Acceptance, however, will force us to face the loss of our old vision of life and the loss of trust in a future we could count on and invest ourselves in. It also means we will be entering the dark canal of rebirth in the eternal creative pattern of life moving forward.

As a boy I remember coming into my room and finding my mother making my bed. This was a time when her cancer was progressing steadily through her body. As she was flapping the sheets, I noticed the tears on her cheeks. I cried out, "Don't worry, I'll do it, let me do it." "No," she responded, "I want to do it." "Why?" I asked. "Because I won't be able to do it much longer," she answered.

She had recognized the necessity of acceptance and that she was changing. Included in these changes were the ways she expressed her love and interests.

Going to ball games and school events, being president of the PTA, and even making our beds—all of the ways she defined herself and found meaning—were ending. Through her courage and wisdom, we were all led to a deeper level of experience and meaning where presence was love and to be alive was the core value supporting this love.

This reflection brings me to another great sacrifice I must make in transformative situations: that of my values. My values are part of the structure that I define myself by and that have guided how I live. They were part of the source of my old dreams for myself, for my loved ones, for my children, for my future, and for a fulfilling life. In transformative situations, they are no longer appropriate for my life. This doesn't mean that I can simply abandon them. It means that my values must evolve and be transformed as I am. If I must learn to say no to people and reject them, or if I must learn to be able to hurt people I love in order to serve a larger vision of life or myself, or if I must stop hiding my pain, illness, and distress in order not to disturb people, then that is what I must do. In fact, once I have such awareness, I will ultimately either do more harm to people or deny them their challenges to grow if I am not faithful to my awareness. If I allow my values to rigidify, they will become another cross that I am nailed to. In my own tree of knowledge that I've worked so hard to nourish is the realization that a value system that is alive…that is transforming… leads to inner confrontations whose flames usher in experiences of depth and love beyond any I could have previously imagined.

We will explore ways of making these sacrifices and restructuring ourselves as this book continues. Because I have a great desire to be fully alive, passion, courage, and fear drive me to search actively into the experiences of my reality. Even in, or perhaps especially in, my dark moments, I find that through this approach, something inside of me begins to shift. I am no longer a victim, and I am beginning to find my own way, and the opportunity to meet resources that are deep in my soul—the ones that can slowly transform my spirit and give me the feeling that I have a center that will support me—ease my fear and bring a certain amount of peace with the realities of my life.

I know this "inner friend" will not rescue me or help me become triumphant, nor will it miraculously cure me or save me from any aspect of the human condition. But it will help me find healing, wholeness, and a renewed love for myself and life. And most of all, it leads me to believe that there is a great kindness hidden in the darkness of the lives we all face. It is my experience of the Divine.

From this point on, I am able to create a perspective that increases my potential for healing and enhances my capacity for life. This is my prayer for my daughter and for everyone. The darkness of illness, pain, suffering, and the loss of our ordinary life takes us out of the conventional world and its goals and values. Once we've turned this corner, we begin to see the world through our own eyes. The art of living and healing begins when what is seen becomes mixed with my depths, my soul. Then new ways of viewing myself in life are revealed, and that is the beginning of the serious art of living. Through the creative power of this art, the tears of my grief and rage become pearls. And my prayers are answered. Radical hope is born.

CHAPTER 1

The Meaning of Radical Hope

Now is the time of dark invitation
Beyond a frontier you did not expect;
Abruptly, your old life seems distant.

— JOHN O'DONOHUE

When I began my reflections in preparation for writing this book, I found myself remembering an afternoon from several winters ago. On that day, I was sitting in my study gazing out at the bleakness and the beauty of the ice that was on our trees. The day reflected my feelings as I was reviewing the impact my daughter's multiple sclerosis (MS) was having on our lives. And I was wondering how many dark nights of the soul can be included in one lifetime. From that gray afternoon until now, I've known that this book isn't a project that I would have chosen to develop. This topic chose me, seized me like a thief in the night. It came out of nowhere and forced me to face it. Radical hope and the healing power of illness are themes that were born out of my experiences with my daughter Marjorie and her struggle against the undertow of multiple sclerosis.

Marjorie had always been strong, very athletic, a healthy eater, and a healthy person. Never in a million years would I have thought that she would encounter a crippling illness like this one. Then, a few years later, while we were still coping with the extent of her pain and limitations, I had to face my own encounter with cancer. As my reflections deepened, I realized that I had faced many problems and adversities in my life, and that during these later years, I had expected my life to be easier—as if I could control and organize my destiny. That's when I discovered, once again, that my life doesn't move according to my plans. That's when I discovered that I am at the mercy of, what…the doctors, luck, old age, God, or the Self—the center of the life force within us? The reality is that this was the beginning of a journey that I am very familiar with. I've been down this road before…because most of our traumas and challenges require a similar psychological and spiritual response.

♦ ♦ ♦

I have come to realize that, in their fundamental nature, the illnesses we have and the illnesses we are, are closely interrelated. Both can direct us toward healing and wholeness, toward living a more complete life. Illnesses intensify our need to focus on the work of creating an environment of healing and wholeness within ourselves. For example, when Ralph had his first heart attack, his world stopped. The same thing happened to Barbara when she was diagnosed with lupus, and also to John when he had his stroke. With Louise, her world slowly ground to a stop with her debilitating experience of fibromyalgia. For all of them, their old selves needed to die along with their old self-images, their ideas of what made up "a good life," and their old dreams of the future.

As I reflected upon the process of "wondering" with Ralph, Barbara, John, and Louise, I realized the way I worked with them was already familiar to me. It was the same way I worked with Charley, whose wife left him unexpectedly when he was sixty. It was the same process I followed with Heather, whose nineteen-year-old son was killed in a car crash. It also had the same components of my work with Bob and Martha, whose business failed in the recession. In many ways, it was the same approach that supported my work with Terrie, who felt trapped and depressed in her job; and my work with Jim, who at age forty-eight began having anxiety attacks that made him wonder what his life was all about. For all of them, their lives needed to be reexamined; old selves needed to die, along with old expectations and dreams. In fact, a total transformation was being called for…but that kind of need is rarely clear at first.

♦ ♦ ♦

I must say, thankfully, that I have been blessed with a strong and healthy body, but I realized that as I got older, someday my turn in the hospital would come. But my daughter Marjorie's illness came as a radical shock that fractured the foundations of my life. And it caused me to ask myself, "What is my life?" I have had difficulties, tragedies, and struggles that shaped me and strengthened me. These battles and challenges made me who I am and channeled my life into the life of a scholar, a seeker, a healer. But seeing my daughter's struggles was an earthquake that shook my foundation.

Marjorie's MS and my cancer brought on the dawning awareness of how much illness had directed the story of my life. This was a staggering realization that almost brought me to my knees. But I have also learned, in my years as a seeker and a healer, that any shock that reverberates from the depth of my soul or from the depth of my experiences in being human will shatter my ideas of what I thought was normal and thought of as conventional wisdom, and then will bring the possibility of new life into being. As we go on through this book, the shattering effects of transformation will be the underlying theme of what I am presenting.

I also had to face the fact—and this is an important point—that whenever we get a significant diagnosis, or when life forces us into a moment of deep self-confrontation, something radical has happened to us, because life as we have known it stops. When I did my own active imagination practices in which I journaled personal, written dialogs directly with my cancer, I found the experience very frightening, difficult, and exhausting. Like others who have gone before me—Kat Duff, John Dunne, and Virginia Woolf—I felt like I had been swallowed into the underworld of illness, seized and possessed and stranded in a wasteland of the soul. And yet, in my better moments, I knew I would not abandon my destiny as a seeker and a healer.

When I learned that I had cancer, it, too, was a bolt out of the blue. One of my worst fears had come true. My body, which I love... that had been strong and had supported me, that bore pain, and that gave me pleasure for many years, was now sick and weak. Like all of us in these kinds of situations, I was dazed by an avalanche of feelings, such as fear, anxiety, betrayal, and jealousy, to name a few, as well as a huge adrenaline reaction. But I soon discovered that what was going on within me was deeper than these emotions and was striking at the foundation of who I am. When these events happen, we lose our framework for who we are, and our self-perception is fractured. The strengths, values, and ideals we have used to structure our self-concept and our self-worth lose their ground, and the structures we have used to plan and envision our hopes and our future crumbles.

As a Jungian analyst, I continue to call this deep pain that accompanies our illnesses "soul-pain." It is pain that comes from feeling betrayed by our bodies, our attitudes, and our ideals. It is pain from the loss of our self-image and the loss of people, things, values, and hopes that are dear to us and cannot be replaced. It is the pain that can scare us into turning against ourselves and that can cause us to see the potential well of strength and direction within our unconscious as threatening rather than supportive. Soul-pain can lead to despair and helplessness. But I have learned something from my experience, and this book's process is designed to help us reengage with the deepest part of ourselves…to come home to ourselves, and to find healing from our grief and relief from our fear.

Every serious diagnosis brings a radical shock to us. Gone are many of the things we identified with to define ourselves, our roles in life, and our vision of the future. Lost, too, are the ideals of our culture that we use, even without knowing it, to characterize our ideas of happiness, well-being, and what makes life worth living. In such a situation, we may soon feel like we are outcasts, people who aren't in control and who aren't productive. We may feel that we have little energy for excess busyness, for making things happen, for having a positive attitude, and for not being a bother to other people. As a result of these discoveries, we are left with secret feelings of shame and failure. And if our illness is acute and life threatening, we are dropped into the instinctual battle between life and death. But if it is chronic and slowly progressive—and even cancer is being considered a chronic illness today—our feelings of shame and failure grow. In both cases, terror lurks beneath the surface of our lives, and our recognizable identity seems burned away and scarred.

As we proceed through this book, we will soon see how radical hope means having the courage to see reality in new ways—to have the courage to face ourselves, to see our reality, our loss—and to proceed through life on a path defined by our soul and not by our family, friends, neighbors, and culture or by our illness.

Figure 1. Tree Roots

Another very important point is that radical hope means finding the inner support rooted within us for creating new attitudes and a new sense of identity—a new self-concept, new self-respect, and deep self-confidence. We have suffered a radical shock, and we are seeking radical hope and a radically new life. The origins of the word "radical" mean having roots below the surface, reaching deep into the earth in a way that is fundamental to life and vital to the soul. As we proceed, we will explore ways to cultivate the roots of this inner support and to create a healing environment within ourselves.

I have also learned bit by bit over the years that radical hope means that challenges, symptoms, and illnesses are not just things to be cured. However, I never underestimate the hope for a cure or a solution, and I support the desire and struggle for all the medical help possible, including what I am proposing. The image of Asclepius, the ancient Greek god of healing, reminds us that in this early, sacred tradition, our symptoms and our illnesses called for a sacred response from us. Such a response begins with choosing not to be a victim and by making a choice that will move us into being a whole new self and living a whole new life, whether we live for a week or decades. As we struggle to live this transforming journey, we will discover that it has a larger spiritual meaning whose goal is the transformation…in fact, the redemption… of our culture—out of the driveness of materialism and busyness and into the values of the heart that define what it means to be truly and fully human.

Our soul-pain…our soul-pain…listen to these words…say them out loud. "Our soul-pain"…isn't that a powerful expression to describe the pain that penetrates us down through our roots? Our soul-pain means we are not only facing an illness or a desperate situation, we are also facing the challenge of bringing forth a new self-identity, of growing a new personality, of helping our old self die, and of encouraging a new self to be born in the midst of our darkest moments. This transformation is a challenging, complicated process, and we know that less than one-third of the people suffering from a serious illness find the inner strength to come through this process well. And only a few caregivers have any real understanding of how to help someone make it through this kind of transformation.

I believe we can do better than we have been doing. That is why I want to begin by presenting a process that starts with acceptance of what we are experiencing and by presenting how to deal with our experiences effectively and creatively. This process offers an outline for having these experiences guide us into the beginning of a new sense of self that:

- **Taps into the wellspring of life, love, and hope within us to guide us to new purpose, to new meaning, and to peace**
- **Increases our healing potential for medical treatment**
- **Increases the general healing environment for our personality**
- **Helps us find a whole new life grounded in love, vitality, and authenticity**
- **Will bring radical hope for our future**

Radical hope means that we can start with loss, pain, despair, anger, and fear and then begin to open the way to becoming conscious of our hidden potentials…to developing them…and to going on to discover the Divine in the Self within ourselves.

This Self (the Great Self or Personality, as Dr. Carl Jung called it) is hidden within us, waiting to be discovered and experienced…and to become engaged in our lives in reality and even during adversity. When we learn through our experiences, this Self is then not merely a lovely psychological or theological idea but is in the center of our lives, if we can come to realize it. When we grow conscious of this inner, higher individuality as the eternal, spiritual core of our being, we come to understand what Dr. Jung meant when he said, "Called or not called, God will be present."

Thoughts and Questions to Ponder...

As you finish reading and reflecting upon this first, intense chapter, find a quiet, comfortable, safe place, and take a few moments to settle in to yourself.

Take some deep breaths, and let me invite you to spend time writing and reflecting in your journal about what you are experiencing with your own illness or the illness of someone close to you, or how you experience illness as a caregiver.

Now, go a bit deeper and journal how you are feeling about your situation or the things you are having to confront and accept.

As you continue to settle deeply into actually feeling your feelings, take time to ask yourself: *Is there is anything getting in the way of me accepting what is happening to me at the present time?*

As you breathe in...pause...and breathe out, place your hand on your heart, and appreciate the emotions you are experiencing... and your capacity to let them just be.

Begin to make peace with your emotions and your breath... relaxing...and simply being centered inside yourself.

Are there any images or thoughts you want to write down to help you remember this sense of being still and quiet within yourself?

Settling into yourself also means having a sense of inner balance.

As you breathe in and breathe out, can you remember a time in your life when you felt a deep sense of inner balance and settledness?

Can you express in your journaling how it felt...how tangible it was?

As you finish reflecting on this chapter, can you begin to let yourself feel more hopeful, and can you start to value your experiences of life in a new way?

Other thoughts...

CHAPTER 2

The Body, Mind, Spirit Connection to Healing

You lived absorbed in the day-to-day,
So continuous with everything around you,
That you could forget that you were separate

— John O'Donohue

In sharing my own approach to illness, I want to begin by explaining more about the Jungian approach to individuation as a way of life. We have all heard about the importance of the body-mind-spirit connection, but few of us know how to deepen that connection beyond trying to change attitudes, developing coping skills, and making often ineffective efforts to free ourselves from the tyranny of complicated lives. Of course, many of these techniques, such as relaxation and mindfulness, are useful and make good starting points, but they are only the beginning of what is needed.

As a culture, we are fond of using labels like chronic illness, acute illness, accidents, trauma, depression, stress, anxiety, eating disorders, and so on. Using labels helps to give us a sense of distance and control. But in reality, we are all vulnerable, and we are all dying, no matter how much we deny death personally. And actually, the more we deny death personally, the more it eventually increases our fear of death, and this fear of death can transmute into a fear of life. The more this fear grows, the more we become deaf and blind to the lessons of our illnesses, our symptoms, and our struggles...and to the lessons of dying itself. We also become mute to their most important lesson—which is to engage in life fully.

In recognition of this reality, the essence of every point I will make throughout this book will concern how we can live more intensely, with more vitality, meaning, and love. If we want to deal with the true depths of our human experiences, we must first understand that a primary reason that we have real trouble with the body-mind-spirit connection is because our culture has not developed the perspective or the concepts necessary to fully understand these connections. We basically have no concepts, no cultural frame of reference, to even ask the kind of intelligent questions that could help us.

We have forgotten da Vinci's renaissance vision of the holistic or quintessential person. The model of thinking and perceiving the world that we are indoctrinated into since our birth is one that is rational and oriented toward establishing cause and effect, defining goals, and pursuing these through goal-oriented behavior. We are also taught to take a pragmatic, problem-solving approach to our lives that turns our illness into medical problems to be managed by health-care professionals.

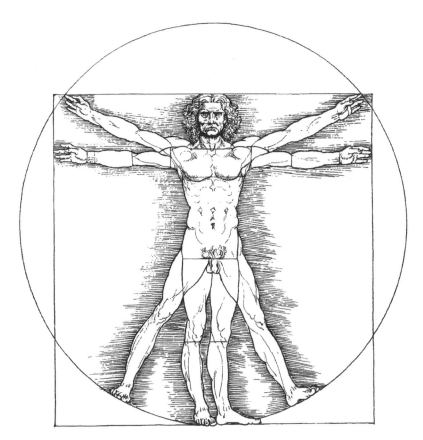

Figure 2. da Vinci's Model

This model is inadequate for experiencing the deep relational patterns within us that support the potential wholeness of body, mind, and spirit. Nor do we adequately understand how we must cultivate our own personalities (our egos, in psychological terms) so they will have the strength for their most important life-giving task. That task is to help us integrate our body, mind, and spirit through the pursuit of self-knowledge and center them in the ground of our being. The world of illness contradicts everything that most of us have learned. Therefore, our healing must become a journey of discovery into these unfamiliar areas. We will explore how we can do that throughout this book.

Being a Rational, Objective, Goal-Oriented, and Problem-Solving Person Isn't Enough

If we want to understand the true depth of our experiences and our potentials to grow and heal, we need to face the ways we have been indoctrinated to think and feel. We need to investigate what has been left out of our collective model of living that is crucial to our well-being, and we must see in how many ways this cultural indoctrination has left us split against ourselves.

Even before I began school, I felt like a misfit in our world, and my experiences in school made me feel even worse. When I first became aware of C. G. Jung's theory of psychological types, I gave a great sigh of relief. I realized that my temperament was exactly the opposite of the style our culture asked us to be. Jung was interested in helping us understand our individual differences by explaining the styles our consciousness takes. For example, we have four complementary ways of interacting with the world, of gathering information, of making decisions, and of organizing our lives. Each complementary set shows two opposite ends on a continuum. In a very oversimplified way, these preferred styles in our personality can be understood in the chart below.

Our personal style is determined by taking the preference we have developed for each item in the four pairs of opposites and then combining them. For example, I am Introverted (I), Intuitive (N), Feeling (F), and Perceiving (P).

I PREFER:

Extroversion (E) The outer world of actions, objects, and persons.	or	**Introversion (I)** The inner world of concepts and ideas.
Sensing (S) The immediate, real, practical facts of experience and life.	or	**Intuition (N)** The possibilities, relationships and meanings of experiences.
Thinking (T) Making decisions objectively and impersonally considering causes of events and where decisions may lead.	or	**Feeling (F)** Making decisions subjectively and personally, weighing values of choices, and how they matter to others.
Judgment (J) Living in a decisive, planned, and orderly way, aiming to regulate and control events.	or	**Perception (P)** Living in a spontaneous, flexible way, aiming to understand life and adapt to it.

I slowly and painfully discovered while growing up that we live in a culture where to achieve success in school and later in work, the core standards for how we approach attaining the "good life" are meant to be goal oriented, rational, analytical, objective, and non-emotional. In this culture, it also helps if we are extroverted and have a positive, can-do attitude. In addition, being objective means being detached, concrete, and factual. In other words, our society tries to indoctrinate us into having an approach to life that looks like this:

Extroverted: Geared to action and the outer world.

Sensation: Emphasis on the concrete, facts, the immediate, the real, and the practical, with linear intuition being accepted.

Thinking: Analysis, objectively considering the facts, impersonal, logical, reductive decision making.

Judgment: Decisive, planned, organized, regulating life, and controlling events.

Thus we are taught to value and develop characteristics that make us one sided and unbalanced. In this process, we have tried our best to repress the other characteristics into our unconscious. Incidentally, Jung's definition of neurosis is to be one sided, and the character of our culture, which has become rigidly one sided in these aspects, can be seen as neurotic.

Another way we can look at how we are split is to use the oversimplified terminology that is commonly referred to as the left brain–right brain division. In this general, oversimplified explanation, our left-brain characteristics are summarized on the left side of the chart of preference, and our right-brain characteristics are listed on the right side. In his excellent book *The Master and His Emissary: The Divided Brain and the Making of the Western World*, Dr. Iain McGilchrist shares a story that provides an analogy of how we have become split against ourselves during the last five hundred years or so in the Western world. The story Dr. McGilchrist uses goes like this:

There was once a wise spiritual Master, who was the ruler of a small but prosperous domain, and who was known for his selfless devotion to his people. As his people flourished and grew in number, the bounds of this small domain spread; and with it, the need to trust implicitly the emissaries he sent to ensure the safety of its ever more distant parts.

It was not that it was just impossible for him personally to order all that needed to be dealt with; as he wisely saw, he needed to keep his distance from, and remain ignorant of such concerns. And so he nurtured and trained carefully his emissaries, in order that they could be trusted. Eventually, however, his cleverest and most ambitious vizier, the one he most trusted to do his work, began to see himself as the Master, and used his position to advance his own wealth and influence. He saw his Master's temperance and forbearance as weakness, not wisdom, and on his missions on the master's behalf, adopted his mantle as his own—the emissary became contemptuous of his Master. And so it came about that the master was usurped, the people were duped, the domain became a tyranny, and eventually it collapsed in ruins.

The point Dr. McGilchrist makes is "that like the Master and his emissary in the story, though the cerebral hemispheres should cooperate, they have for some time been in a state of conflict. Currently, in our society, we are in the hands of the vizier (the detached, rational, goal-oriented, pragmatic approach to life)," who, however gifted, is, in effect, an ambitious regional bureaucrat with his own interest at heart. Meanwhile, the Master, the one whose wisdom gave the people peace and security, is led away in chains. The Master is betrayed by his emissary. In our book *Into the Heart of the Feminine* that my wife, Massimilla, and I coauthored, we explain that like the emissary, the pragmatic, rational approach to life has become dominant in our cultural institutions. It has become the definition of what we call "patriarchal."

When I was recovering from my cancer surgery in the hospital, the healing experience there was abysmal. It was not a healing atmosphere of caring, quiet, receptivity, and safety. In other words, there were none of the healing principles of the great archetypal feminine present in that institutional setting. I left the hospital much more depleted than I should have. Such a "patriarchal" setting will not become truly healing until there is a fundamental change in the mentality of the institution. This change requires a basic shift in our consciousness that includes and values the feminine principle. It will never come from endless surveys on patient satisfaction designed by the system at fault.

When we become rational and objective, we can become detached not only from our experience of life but even from our capacities to experience life. This kind of approach leaves us suffering from a *plague of disengagement*. Medical and other professional caregivers often don't want to and don't know how to listen to their patients. When the emissary is in charge in our mind, we don't even want to listen to our own pain and suffering or to understand them; nor do we, meaning not only caregivers but also ourselves, want to listen to the pain and suffering of others, and we don't want to take the time to understand them.

The heart of our problem is really centered on our unwillingness to seek the ways we need to know to actually heal ourselves so that our wholeness can become the foundation of new cultural attitudes. Dr. Jung was clear when he wrote, "The psychological rule says that when an inner situation is not made conscious, it happens outside as fate." This rule is just as true for us collectively as it is individually. I suffered this fate in the hospital individually because we have been unwilling to face our disengagement from our whole selves.

As we look at this picture, we can also say that our world of values, feelings, emotions, and purpose in life are now taken for granted, rather than being explored and cultivated. Without cultivation, we easily lose touch with this world. The emotions—that can lead us to commitment, inspiration, and passion, as well as to our deepest values, and our intuition, which can give us a vision of hope for the future—are bound in chains. Our capacities to be introverted, to be reflective, and to seek true wisdom, which are positive characteristics of the archetypal feminine principle, are also bound in chains. As we continue in this book, we will see how this one-sided approach inhibits our efforts at healing as well as our efforts to bring our body, mind, and spirit into a vital, healing relationship.

Two Healing Environments: The Outer and the Inner

When I consider our approaches to healing, I also think about how these two different yet often intertwined environments—the inner and the outer—affect our efforts to heal and thrive. We all know that if we are breathing polluted air and drinking contaminated water, we are going to get sick. We also know that we need to eat healthy food, get good exercise, and get plenty of sleep. Yet in too many cases, some force within us or without—that we may categorize as demands, busyness, and even the results of our values—keeps us from giving ourselves the healthy environment that we need.

During the last five hundred years, when the Master in our story has become imprisoned, some of our deepest values have gone with him. In the Middle Ages, when people believed in God, many indigenous people then still believed that everything had a soul that could speak to our soul and move us toward a love of life. Today our so-called materialism sees everything as an object to be used in pragmatic, utilitarian, or self-enhancing ways. Without the influence of the Master, we fail to see our homes as sacred places inviting us to live in them… our workplaces as sacred places inviting us to work in them…and feel at home and good in them. And perhaps worst of all, we see our bodies mechanically, as things to be "tuned up" and "fixed," not as the sacred vessels to carry our souls through life.

What is even more difficult for us is to understand that we must create an inner environment that supports our growth, our ability to thrive, and our healing. At the end of his book, Dr. McGilchrist suggests that the way to return the Master to his rightful place, the way to heal and transcend the split in our minds, is through the pursuit of the kind of self-knowledge that leads us to a still-further state of heightened consciousness. Dr. Carl Jung's approach to bringing our lives healing, wholeness, and growth leads us to this state of illuminated consciousness where body, mind, and spirit interact in a container of wholeness.

The Jungian Approach

I have loved the Jungian approach since I first discovered it, because it is radically different and far more profound than our conventional and even our alternative approaches to our problems, struggles, dysfunctions, and illnesses. The Jungian perspective is that our suffering and struggles become meaningful parts of our lives when they are understood and when we come to the realization that they can initiate us into a more profound sense of being and satisfaction. The term Dr. Jung developed—**individuation**—is how we describe the process of our journey into wholeness and authenticity.

In fact, individuation is the centerpiece of the Jungian legacy. It is a path that shows us how developing self-knowledge helps the most difficult encounters with ourselves and life, and how these encounters become the building blocks of our inner strength and a fulfilled life. We can then say that, like the stone the builders rejected, our most challenging experiences, our frustrating complexes, and most assuredly our illnesses can become our teachers, and they hold the greatest promise for expanding our personalities and our lives.

In his Zarathustra lectures, Dr. Jung explains to us that our life and our individual consciousness only progress by a continuous series of pregnancies and births, transformations—giving rebirth to ourselves. And illness asks us to be more devoted to this process. When I was struggling through my own midlife conflicts and confrontations with family illnesses, I sadly discovered that my efforts to become at home with the deeper dimensions of life, which included my efforts to see my failures, conflicts, and sufferings as teachers, had an unexpected side.

These struggles that were leading me into the heart of an authentic life were also threatening to my ideals and fantasies of a "good life," a productive life, as well as to my longings for peace, love, and security. This unconventional approach also threatened many of the people close to me and their conventional values of trying to fix things, to get back to normal, and to get on with life. For those of us with chronic illnesses, it means we must always struggle to not become victims of the continuous outer pressures of family, health-care establishments, and society to define ourselves as a "patient" and become trapped in that role. We must undertake the healing journey that I will soon describe to create a new environment within ourselves that fosters restoration and growth.

Dr. Jung's radical approach, which requires that we reeducate ourselves, is backed by sound theory and almost a hundred years of experience. It can guide us in learning how to face our challenges and unleash their transformative powers in a way that renews our energy, reconnects us to its source, and enables our enlarged personalities to become the cornerstone of a more vital life. Dr. Jung assures us, "Creating—that is the great salvation from suffering and life's alleviation. But for the creator to appear, suffering itself is needed, and much transformation."

Each true rebirth in life is preceded by a dark night of the soul. As a result of this reality, the goal of Jungian psychology is never to get back to normal. It is always to grow through our problems **to a place beyond normal**. It is to use what we call the *transcendent function* in our personality. That means to hold the tension of the conflicts in our suffering. In the case of illness, it means the tension of our recognition of how we are and our longing to be the way we were. It also means the tension between our pain and our fear, especially our soul-pain, until the transcendent function—which we often know as grace—moves us to a new place due to our journey into our own depths of feeling and into our unconscious.

Now the question I am concerned with is, "How do we do this in the midst of an illness...particularly when terror or pain have brought our instinctual selves and the concerns for our own survival to the forefront of our lives?" We will begin to answer that question with my discussion of "acceptance" in the next chapter.

Thoughts and Questions to Ponder...

In your journey to discover unfamiliar territory within you, write down three times in your life that you had an experience that you feel you are still "working on"...

Take experience #1 and write in a few sentences:

- How you emotionally responded to this experience
- How your body felt during the experience, and afterward
- What your mind thought about the experience
- How you felt on a soul level

Take experience #2 and write in a few sentences:

- How you emotionally responded to this experience
- How your body felt during the experience, and afterward.
- What your mind thought about the experience
- How you felt on a soul level

Take experience #3 and write in a few sentences:

- How you emotionally responded to this experience
- How your body felt during the experience, and afterward
- What your mind thought about the experience
- How you felt on a soul level

Other thoughts...

CHAPTER 3

Beyond Normal:
Transformation Comes After Acceptance

In the name of the Fire,
The Flame
And the Light
Praise the pure presence of fire
That burns from within
Without thought of time.

            – JOHN O'DONOHUE

As I began thinking about radical acceptance and transformation, I was reminded of the time when Beth came in to see me. Beth was in her early forties, and she sat down and softly began to tell me about her experience with multiple sclerosis (MS). This was only a couple of years after my daughter's diagnosis and still in the period when we were realizing the depth and seriousness of her illness. I felt nailed to my chair as Beth began by telling me she had read my newsletters about my daughter and me. Then, as she was talking, she began quietly weeping. I noticed that even in her sadness, she was well dressed and didn't look sick. I soon found out that three years into her illness, she was now experiencing fatigue, one leg was getting difficult to control, and lesions on her brain were keeping her from performing her former profession. Beth was married and had two children. Fear and stress, feelings that I have learned to experience very well, were a constant undercurrent in her family and in her life.

As she told me her story, she confessed to how long she had ag-onized over what she might have done to cause her MS. Quietly she said, "I was so relieved, so freed up to hear that you don't buy the idea that we cause our illnesses." Of course, Beth is right. Our culture is stuck in cause-and-effect, black-and-white thinking, in what I call patriarchal or left-brain thinking. In addition, even many of our new age, alternative approaches tend to teach us that if we have the right beliefs, attitudes, affirmations, and so on, we won't get sick. Or if we have the right belief systems, we can cure anything or manifest a return to health. That's *wrong*, and that's magical thinking. There are many factors in every illness. Even the right diet and exercise that promote health don't guarantee that we won't get sick.

It seems as if our scientific, rational, technological approach during the last century or two has given us the mistaken idea that we can get rid of the painful aspects of life, our illnesses, and our suffering—things we don't like or that fail to make our life easy and that don't fit into the realm of our power and control. Rationality creates its own shadow side of blindness, and our marketing institutions are quick to take advantage of these blind spots. We seem to think we can live happily ever after through willpower, technology, or the right self-help or diet formula. Our marketing institutions are also quick to take advantage of our fears, unhappiness, and desires for a better life by burying us in an avalanche of self-help and diet books with their seven-step formulas that, with willpower, promise us that love, empowerment, and health will be ours. Not many of our books or teachers are challenging us to look deeper into our unconscious, where the Master, the feminine principle, and our souls are chained...or to look into the dungeon, where the possibility of transformation and healing is really hidden. This book is going to do that.

My daughter was a great athlete, and I am intensely proud of her accomplishments. And of course, I've heard some people say almost smugly or knowingly that she must have exhausted her body, or "What was she running away from through her exercise?" There is a special cruelty in these kinds of statements. In fact, they are fear-based responses reflecting the deep fear and defensiveness residing in the people making them. These people miss the true meaning of our experiences because of their deep unconscious fear of encountering what it means to be truly human. They smother the potential in how much we can learn from our suffering, our illnesses, and our struggles; how much we can change who and what we are as a result of this learning; and how we can find new hope, love, and purpose. They fail to realize this learning speaks to the potential in the human spirit, not to the idea that we somehow failed and caused our illness.

◆ ◆ ◆

A few sessions later, when Beth came into my office, she began by saying, "You know, I haven't told you, but I have really been angry with you for a couple of weeks." "Oh, can you tell me why?" I asked. "You bet!" she answered. "I read your piece about acceptance, and it made me furious. I've always been taught to have a positive attitude and believe that I could overcome my illness, beat it, or pray it away; or do enough work on my diet, health, and emotions to make it go away; or reach a point of psychological health where I wouldn't need it anymore; or I would find the right treatment to defeat it. How can I be expected to accept something I'm terrified of, that is ruining my life? If I accept it, I will have nothing left but anger and despair."

Then she paused. And after sitting quietly for a few moments, absorbing this mouthful and knowing just how she was feeling, I said, "Please go on."

"Well," she said, "after journaling about my anger, I realized that there was more to your article. I realized that acceptance isn't surrender. It is to accept the reality of the present moment, to let my old notions of fighting and overcoming it die, and this does two things. First, it opens the space for transformation to begin. Second, it allows me to take a breath and say this illness is part of who I am, but it will not define who I am." Then I thanked her, and I felt we had turned a major corner in her journey.

In his now-famous *Red Book*, his life-changing personal journal, Dr. Jung explains how very difficult it was for him to break free from the spirit of his times.

It is just as hard for us to open the cage of our own indoctrination. And that is the cage of black-and-white thinking, having a positive attitude, and being rational. This is the cage we were born and raised in. As we begin to consider our lives more seriously, we must be careful to remember that accepting our illness doesn't mean giving up or giving into it, nor does it mean embracing it or loving it. After all, the princess didn't embrace the frog in the fairy tale; she kissed it. And a kiss is a transformative act in fairy tales.

Figure 3. Woman in a Cage

I find it helpful to realize that we didn't choose to grow up in this cage. I like to think what happened to us early in our lives goes something like this. Imagine our life is threatened, and in order to escape the threat, we must create another identity, a false cover. In a way, this is what most of us do as we grow up and seek to fit into the world. Most of us are familiar with some of the false identities we both create and live within that began in our early childhood as we sought safety and as we sought to fit in and to be appreciated. Several examples of our false identities that come to mind are the people pleaser, the perfectionist, the rebel, the workaholic, the high achiever, the eternal adolescent, and the shy, hidden type of person. You can probably think of more.

It is very helpful for us to remember that if we need to fight, defeat, or overcome an illness, symptom, or even an attitude or characteristic, we have actually made it into an enemy and are losing the value of the potential it can guide us toward. Our approach on this journey is to work in a way that is constructive—that stands for and cultivates growth and transformation that will strengthen and empower us. Warfare drains us and should be chosen very carefully. Even when I've taken an antibiotic to "kill" an infection, or when I had my cancer surgically removed, I did not consider myself at war with either the infection or the cancer. I believe that I was helping my body heal, and that infections and cancers can still be great teachers. A good example of this point is our experience of the common cold. We all know that we live in a body and a world that are full of viruses. The question is, what makes us susceptible to a virus? Generally, the answer is stress and fatigue. Once we have the virus, what helps us recover from it? The answer, which is obvious, is deep rest. To help our body resist a virus and recover from one, we must learn how important rest is to our bodies.

Again and again, Jung emphasizes in his writings that nothing can be transformed until it is accepted. And this acceptance of ourselves is absolutely necessary for us to become whole and to be able to nurture, support, and work in partnership with ourselves. At one point during our sessions, Beth reflected, "Accepting myself is also difficult because it means on different days I'm angry, frustrated, or in despair, or hopeful—or my emotions are on a roller coaster I can't control." There is no doubt that acceptance also means to accept what we are feeling even in our darkest moments of anger, fear, despair, and hopelessness. Once again, Dr. Jung is helpful as he tells us how to handle our dark moments: "I should advise you to put it all down as beautifully as you can—in some beautifully bound book." Jung continues, "It will seem as if you were making the visions banal—but then you need to do that—then you are freed from the power of them...then when these things are in some precious book you can go to the book and turn over the pages and for you it will be your church—your cathedral—the silent places in your spirit where you will find renewal. If anyone tells you that it is morbid or neurotic and you listen to them—you will lose your soul—for in that book is your soul."

Figure 4. The Phoenix

For myself, I call my book my *Darkness Journal.* I will share some of my writings about cancer from this journal later in this book. It is in this journal that I learn through my weaknesses, through my ignorance…that I learn of my previously unknown strengths and potentials and how to appreciate them. I also discover that as I separate from my feelings by writing them out in a special place, I can relate to them more objectively, heal them, and learn from them. In this precious journal, I have learned to become a compassionate witness to myself as I weep my tears, feel my sorrows, and admit my fear and my rage at life, my illness, my daughter's illness, and fate. In addition, through it, I see how life is beginning to uncover my depths, hone my strengths, and initiate me into the truth of my soul's identity…and uncover the bone-deep wisdom in my greater Self. This process is one that has taken me beyond my horizons to places that I never could have imagined. Acceptance is a radical idea that has opened me to the nest of fire and ashes inside of me—the nest that contains all the necessary ingredients to give rise to a phoenix of new life within me.

Thoughts and Questions to Ponder...

Before we can approach dealing with the reality of our illness, it is important to honor and acknowledge the state of shock we may still be in concerning our diagnosis. Often we feel shaken to the core of our being.

Take some moments to actually feel the shock that you may still be feeling through your body.

Begin to let it go…

Take time to write a few words (a few scribbles, lines, or pictures) of how you are experiencing this shock and how you are letting it go.

Take time to journal how you feel inside when you say each of these sentences:

I am willing to acknowledge the shock I felt.

I am willing to feel how I feel…even though I may still be experiencing shock.

I acknowledge that I may have experienced many levels and layers of shock.

I am willing to breathe in…to pause…to breathe out…to pause… and to breathe in again…

Even though I feel that the very foundation of "who I am" has been shaken, I am willing to feel myself at the very core of my being, the core of my foundation.

Before "diagnosis," we live in what we could call "the ordinary world"…full of activities, working, living life with family and friends.

This ordinary world includes our ideas about our identity, our place in life, our personal values, our goals. We generally live under the spell of what is called "normal"…"wanting the good life"…and relying on "conventional wisdom."

Our thoughts and visions of the future, our hopes, and our dreams take place in the context of this "ordinary, normal world."

After "diagnosis," we have the possibility of seeing "beyond normal" and of regarding our illness as a "sacred call."

When I consider the possibility that through my illness, my body is asking for a sacred response from me...what are my feelings about this? How can I continue to explore this question?

Here are my thoughts and feelings about each of these sentences from chapter 3:

"I realized that acceptance isn't surrender."

"Acceptance...is to accept the reality of the present moment, to let my old notions of fighting and overcoming it [the illness] die...

...and this does two things. First, it opens the space for transformation to begin.

Second, it allows me to take a breath and say this illness is part of who I am, but it will not define who I am."

Other thoughts...

CHAPTER 4

The Power of Choosing Life

As air intensifies the hunger of fire,
May the thought of death
Breathe new urgency
Into our love of life.

— John O'Donohue

We find through Dr. Jung's suggestions that we are making a radical choice when we confront our darkest moments and feelings in our own Darkness Journal. And he is assuring us that if we pursue this work religiously, a sacred space and influence will evolve from this work into our lives. I have always been deeply moved by Jung's statement shortly before his death, when he said: "To this day, God is the name by which I designate all things which cross my willful path violently and recklessly, all things which upset my subjective views, plans and intentions and change the course of my life for better or worse." This statement is saturated with the kind of meaning that demands serious understanding—in other words, our most careful attention.

Dr. Jung goes on to remind us that we have an inner guide that can lead us, an inner friend that can support us, and an inner aspect of the Divine that will help bring new vitality, vision, and resilience into our lives. These resources don't just pop up. We must choose to seek them, to be open to them, and to welcome them. Dr. Jung describes this inner friend and guide as the Self. In Dr. Jung's terminology, the word Self is capitalized in order to distinguish it from what we think of as our everyday self or, in psychoanalytic terms, our ego. I am going to call them our big Self and our little self.

The big Self, though, is much more than a friend and guide. It also stands for the archetypal image of our fullest potentials and the unity of our personality as a whole. As the unifying principle in our personality, it therefore represents the central position of authority in relation to our psychological life and personal destiny. In addition to containing the pattern of our potentials and the life we are to fulfill in our unique way, the big Self also contains the creative life force that seeks to compel our growth. This life force will attempt to lure us or push us toward wholeness—toward the completion of our pattern or potentials. If we are strongly on the wrong track with our life or caught in the shell of a rigidified life, the big Self will seek to crack this shell, and it may use an illness to accomplish this cracking open.

In this case, our illness is not our enemy. It is the alarm system going off through our spirit, mind, and body connections, telling us we are living in a self-destructive way, oblivious to or even against the patterns of our potentials and our own life force. In these situations, we must learn to try to listen to the big Self as it is trying to communicate with us through our emotions, life events, dreams, and symptoms. If we don't learn how to listen to our inner alarm system, it will repeat itself more and more seriously until it is heard or it is too late. I will share a map and method for this kind of listening in the second half of the book.

Because of this inherent power in the big Self, which is so integral to our lives, I consider it as the central core of our lives. Because it is demanding to be recognized within each of us in the Western tradition, we often refer to it as the "image of God within us." For me, it has been the source of what I consider my experiences of the Divine. In the Buddhist tradition, it might be a metaphor for enlightenment or "Buddha consciousness." Many of the great religions have the goal of bringing unity to the personality and consciousness, from the psychological perspective.

The reality is that if we are going to realize our full growth and live our unique life…if we are going to create an inner environment of growth, healing, and love…and if we are going to achieve a true sense of peace and strength, then at some point in our life, we must become aware of the existence of this deeper center within us—the big Self that contains a greater intellect and vitality than our ego, our little self or everyday personality. Dr. Jung was fond of saying that "if we do not carefully heed life's hints, then life will hit us in the face." In other words, healing and growth come not only from taking life's hints but from conscientiously making the inner journey that is necessary to help us discover the blueprint of our potentials. Then we consciously participate in moving the contents of our unconscious, as they are presented by the big Self, one by one into our conscious personality in order to refine them and live them. True healing can only come from within.

The availability of this inner wealth at many times and in different circumstances in our lives means that choice isn't a simple one-time event—choice is an evolving journey. Starting this journey as a seeker is a turning point.

Figure 5. Woman Stepping out of Cage

If we can open the door of our cage of traditional thinking and step outside of it, we find opportunity and hope. Let me say this again, as strongly as I can: we must choose to be seekers of new and deeper self-knowledge and consciousness, rather than allow ourselves to become passive in the face of our lives and slip into hollow versions of our potential selves. This choice to be a seeker won't work without practice. Like any spiritual path or physical training program, one must practice it regularly, even when it makes us sore or seems discouraging. The more we do it, the more depth and strength we gain. The more power we give to the process and the more we invest in it, the larger the return is for us. This work isn't easy, but anything worth having...worth treasuring... means that we need to "show up." To choose life means to commit to the journey...to be dedicated...to go deep enough within ourselves to touch the life force within us...to love it, to listen to it, and to let it love us.

The Jungian analyst Guy Corneau spent *two years* dialoging (a method we will cover in this book) with his cancer cells, which also means listening to them, every day. For treating back pain and other illnesses, Dr. John Sarno, in his book *The Divided Mind*, gives a protocol of inner work for forty minutes a day *for months*. In dialoging and listening to my cancer, it told me how I was blocking my life force and creativity. You may be sure that this was a scary and difficult process for me. It was even more difficult to get my head around the idea that an illness that was so frightening to me could be telling me how I need to transform myself and redirect my life. When we are conditioned to act as chronic cases or to see ourselves as impaired or damaged, we give our authority over to others and/or decide to defensively disassociate from our illness. All too often, society will support our making a decision to take on a "positive attitude" that can cause us to be more pleasing to people while we are actually spending the rest of our lives as shadow versions of our former selves.

Becoming a seeker is a choice that we are often forced to make in the halls of fear and loss and in a world filled with pain, blood, sweat, and tears. But in my experience, in the long run, nothing is more destructive than self-alienation, than feeling powerless, hopeless, and unloved by myself and the Divine. By having the courage to accept my reality, I have taken a great step forward as a seeker. When I go into the darkness of this reality, something deep inside of me begins to shift, and I am no longer a victim. I am beginning to find my way and to meet resources deep within myself that can slowly transform my spirit and give me the feeling that I have an inner friend—the big Self—

Figure 6. The Seeker

that will support me, ease my fear, and bring me a certain amount of peace. It will not rescue me or help me become triumphant, but it will guide me through the darkness and into healing and wholeness.

One day Beth said to me that "getting back to normal is never going to happen. If we think it will happen or can happen, we are in denial. Even if my physical symptoms miraculously stopped, I have been forever changed emotionally and spiritually. I could never be the naïve, trusting, driven person I was before." And she is right.

In the face of a demanding illness, our fears, time pressures, exhaustion, lack of skills, and lack of models of transformation discourage us from becoming seekers. These lacks also discourage us from asking ourselves the archetypal questions—the Grail questions that the knight Parsifal had to learn to ask in the legends of King Arthur and the search for the Holy Grail.

We will explore these questions later in the book and see how they can help lead us to a creative transformation that will give us hope and strength, even if it doesn't lead to a cure. Far too many people I have worked with have been forced into desperation before they became seekers. In fact, it was that way for me. However, if we can open our eyes, it may not have to be that way. I would like to urge you to please start now to awaken to your big Self, to build a healing environment within you, to discover the healing possibilities within you, to discover the power of your own life force. Choose life and love—it's your choice.

Thoughts and Questions to Ponder…

A commitment is a love story.

Committing to your self…your own authentic self…is the beginning of the most important story of your life…a story of loving yourself as a sacred commitment…

This ongoing love story of truly valuing yourself opens the way for you to love all that is…to love your big Self…and to embrace what is true and to actively seek your full participation in it.

What does making a commitment to your own journey of healing feel like?

Notice how it feels to announce each of these sentences below to yourself:

I commit to being fully human.

How does it feel to say this…do you have any resistances?

*I accept that I am experiencing this illness, and
I commit to being open to my own transformation.*

How does it feel to say this…do you have any resistances?

*I choose to be a seeker of new and deeper
self-knowledge and consciousness.*

How does it feel to say this…do you have any resistances?

*I embark on my journey…and bring my resolve, my willingness
to stay the course, to be my true, authentic self…*

How does it feel to say this…do you have any resistances?

*I commit myself to be and do what is best for me…to nurture love,
patience, persistence, acceptance, and respect for myself.*

How does it feel to say this…do you have any resistances?

How does this level of loving yourself and caring about yourself feel to you?

Other thoughts…

CHAPTER 5

A Wholistic, Integrated Approach

Now this dark companion has come between you.
Distances have opened in your eyes.
You feel that against your will
A stranger has married your heart.

— JOHN O'DONOHUE

By discussing acceptance as well as the power of choice and transformation as I have been doing, I am beginning to bring not only Jungian psychology into the healing process picture but am also bringing in the discussion of ancient, very time honored practices as well. Two of these are clearly emphasized in the healing model of the ancient Greeks. From his experience as a hospice physician, Dr. Michael Kearney, in his book ***A Place of Healing: Working with Nature and Soul at the End of Life***, names these Hippocratic Medicine and Asklepion Healing.

Historically, Hippocrates was the founder of medicine, while Asclepius was the Greek god of healing. In this illustration, figure 7, you see a very interesting picture of Asclepius and his daughter Hygeia. In other depictions he is seen leaning on the club that belonged to Heracles, which is entwined by the snake as a symbol of healing. The club rests on the head of a bull,

Figure 7. Asclepius & Hygeia

representing life's instinctual power. And we often see Telesphorus, the son of Asclepius, whose name means completion. In other pictures of Hygeia, she is pictured as the Greek goddess of healing, and her name means health. She is often shown leaning on a tripod, which evokes the Delphic Apollo and is entwined by the same snake. She is frequently accompanied by the god Eros. This very intricate illustration of archetypal healing energies shows the complexities and depths of our own healing potentials. My point here is to emphasize that I am not offering an alternative approach to illness. I am trying to revitalize a wholistic approach to well-being.

A Wholistic Approach

As we begin to talk about a truly wholistic approach to healing, let's begin by looking at a painting by the sixteen-year-old Picasso titled *Science and Caritas*. For a few minutes, let yourself ponder the combination of science and caring shown by a young Picasso. With this background in mind, let me return to my story about Beth.

On her second visit with me, Beth began to pour out a long account of her experiences with healers. She told me how angry she had been with doctors or nurses who seemed abrupt, impatient, or even too flippant about something, or were simply unable to help her. She also explained how many alternative healers, therapists, and counselors she had been to since her illness began. Some of these helped her for short periods of time, but then she often felt betrayed, as if they were just out for the money. But she also noted that one of them had referred her to me.

My heart was touched as I listened to her, because my daughter and I had walked that path. As our discussion continued, I shared that overall, my experience with my doctors was very good. However, I also shared that I have had many experiences like hers. When people in the medical community are frustrated, I have seen them blame the patient and create a fear-based approach to healing. I went on to explain to Beth that our problem is that we still haven't worked out an approach to illness that serves our best ideals of compassion and healing. Nor have we worked out a model that supports our caregivers and gives them a valid way to approach patients who are choosing death over life in the ways they act and refuse to change while at the same time blaming their caregivers because they aren't getting better. I can assure you that analysts also have some of these experiences.

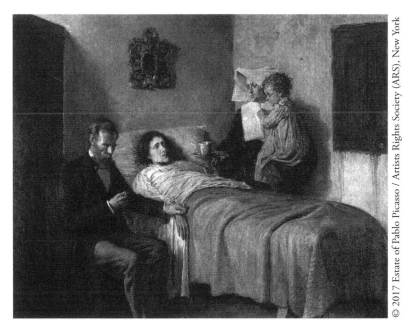

Figure 8. Science and Caritas by Picasso

Most of us are also aware of how our one-sided and too often financial, bottom-line approach to treatments is squeezing our primary care physicians. It is hindering their efforts to have the time to truly listen to their patients and to take the time to truly discover the full picture of the symptoms they are having. Nor do they have the time to help their patients feel really understood and cared about. This pressure sabotages the building of a healing relationship. All too often physicians are not even very well trained in the art of setting up a healing relationship and thereby activating the healing potentials in the patient that could support and enhance their treatments.

In the case of our hospitals, the one-sided, bottom-line approach causes staff to be stretched too thin, and nurses are often placed in areas where they haven't specialized. When I had my surgery for prostate cancer, my nurse had been shifted to cover from another area, or from a pool, and wasn't knowledgeable about urology. When I began to have severe bladder spasms which were extremely painful, she began giving me morphine until she couldn't give me any more. My pain had not abated at all, and I insisted that she get her supervisor. Her supervisor knew exactly what to do and gave me an antispasmodic medication that worked quickly. But I had suffered needlessly for some time, my stitches had torn loose, and it took several additional weeks for my healing.

In my mind, the wrong values are running our health-care system. My nurse had no ill intentions. She simply hadn't been trained in the area where she was placed. I know from my clinical work with hospital staff members that they also feel overstressed, frustrated, and generally unhappy in their professions. In addition, staff such as chaplains who provide caring support to patients and hospital employees are being drastically cut and stretched very thin. The reality is that we have serious, collective problems in our health-care system, and we are keeping our heads in the sand instead of facing them.

In far too many cases of chronic illness and emotional situations, our health-care system continues to contribute toward making the patient feel alienated from our general culture, like a leper. And what is even more important, it doesn't know how to recognize the profound meaning in every illness and its direct reflection on *what we are*, personally and culturally. Nor does it have any real idea of how to help us create an inner environment for healing and growth.

Then, as Beth and I continued to talk, I shared with her how Dr. Jung had electrified me with his position that our mistakes, neurosis, complexes, addictions, and illnesses are much more than shameful, negative, unfortunate characteristics or events that we need to ferret out, overcome, or get rid of. He considered these things that we usually dislike about ourselves or despise as part of life as containers of a divine spark. At first, they appear as blocks to our development, such as the achievement of our goals, hopes, plans, or dreams. But within these very blocks are the seeds, even the road maps and the energy, that, when tapped, can lead us to authenticity and our ability to live as fully as possible. This is a radical approach but not an entirely new one.

As I was reflecting on Beth's frustrating journey with healers, I began to jot down a few notes to clarify my own thoughts. It is apparent to me that if we really want to have a wholistic approach to our illnesses, one that combines body, mind, and spirit, we must understand the two approaches that Dr. Kearney explains. I also think that it is important for us to understand that Dr. Jung's psychology of healing and wholeness is bringing the Asklepion approach to healing into today's language and practices while clearly respecting the Hippocratic approach, or what we now call allopathic medicine. In simple terms, I believe Hippocratic medicine begins with the rational approach to illness that becomes the foundation of evidence-based medicine upon which our current medical model rests. I see it as an attempt to develop a rational and effective approach for understanding our illnesses. In addition, it bases medical theory on the careful observation of concrete reality and making a rational diagnosis within a given theory of disease. This model exploded with the expansion of science and technology in the last few centuries and has been very powerful.

Because the Hippocratic model is based on concrete and observable reality, it intervenes from the outside of the patient, treats an illness as a problem to be solved, and requires objectivity, and its basic training focuses on concrete knowledge and skills. Its effectiveness rests on how well this knowledge is applied. Its goal is a return to normal functioning for the patient. But make no mistake about it—even though a doctor may be interested, kind, and dedicated, emotions and subjective factors are not a real part of this Hippocratic, allopathic model, and they can be regarded as dangerous at times. Even medical centers and programs that consider healing touch, massage, meditation, and support groups as useful keep these factors secondary and want them to be shoehorned into the allopathic model, which reduces them to being just other tools in the current treatment process. While physicians still give lip service to the idea that they are helping the body heal, they are taking the approach of the "emissary" in Dr. McGilchrist's story and are leaving the "Master" hopelessly chained and out of the picture. But we ourselves can help return the Master and the Asklepion approach to the realm of contemporary healing.

Figure 9. Model of the Asklepion at Epidaurus, Greece, 1936

I had to look back into the history of ancient Greece to find the bare bones of the Asklepion model, as well as more information about the divine mentor of healing, Asclepius. The ancient Greeks, who were not religious in the ways we think of as being religious, knew, however, that there were deep forces operating in our lives that determined our fate...and that we had little knowledge of. They also knew that our lack of awareness of these forces could lead us to a tragic fate, including an illness. They often referred to these forces as a god or goddess. Our lack of awareness today puts us at the mercy of forces beyond our control. Our loss of this perspective prompted Dr. Jung to write, in *Man and His Symbols*, "The motto, 'where there is a will, there's a way' is the superstition of modern man. Yet in order to sustain his creed, contemporary man pays the price in a remarkable lack of introspection. He is blind to the fact that, with all his rationality and efficiency, he is possessed by 'powers' that are beyond his control. His gods and demons have not disappeared at all; they have merely got new names. They keep him on the run with restlessness, vague apprehensions, psychological complications, an insatiable need for pills, alcohol, tobacco, food—and, above all, a large array of neuroses" (p. 82) We have now learned that this price is also a contributor to most of our major illnesses. The Jungian approach to healing helps us update and revitalize the Asklepion approach to healing, which includes making us aware of the unseen forces that are working within us and reconnecting us to the Master, the Self, the life force, and potentials below the surface of our lives.

As we start this journey of renewal, let us look into this history. In the tradition of Asclepius, the patients had to come to a temple of Asclepius for healing in order to begin in a sacred space. After entering the temple, the patients went through a series of rituals to put them in the right frame of mind for healing. In this Asklepion tradition, **healing begins within us**. It happens from the inside out and is stimulated by rituals that touch the depths of human experience that connect us with the deep healing potentials in our unconscious. These potentials are mobilized through dreaming, ritual activities, and the images that may arise in our imaginations.

Figure 10. Patient Lying on a Couch with Asclepius

Clearly, this approach uses our subjective experiences of feelings, instincts, imagination, and intuition, and our deepening awareness of our bodies. It assumes that while suffering can diminish, damage, and even destroy us, there is also a potential for transformation and wholeness in it. In other words, in the Asklepion tradition, illness and suffering are an ongoing initiation if we can become aware of their potentials. We remember that Beth said that she would never be the same person again, even if she were instantly cured. It is not surprising that the core of training for this approach is self-knowledge and a broad knowledge of the human experience. The primary requirement for those of us who practice this kind of healing is to be fully engaged in a continuously evolving process of developing self-knowledge. In particular, it means the experience of journeying into our own suffering and learning to listen to and work with our deep inner nature, including the messages from our bodies.

In the history of medicine, Asclepius was the patron of physicians as well as patients. This approach emphasizes that when working with people who are sick or suffering, the personhood of the caregiver is an essential part of the healing process. In becoming Jungian psychoanalysts, we are taught that the whole personalities of the analyst and analysand are called into play. In his autobiography, *Memories, Dreams, Reflections*, Dr. Jung, who was also a medical doctor, writes, "There are many cases which the doctor cannot cure without committing himself. When important matters are at stake, it makes all the difference whether the doctor sees himself as a part of the drama, or cloaks himself in his authority. In the great crises of life, in the supreme moments when to be or not to be is the question, little tricks of suggestion do not help. Then the whole being of the doctor is challenged…The doctor is effective only when he himself is affected. 'Only the wounded physician heals.' But when the doctor wears his personality like a coat of armor, he has no effect." For this reason, as part of our professional training as Jungian psychoanalysts, we are required to go through an extensive personal training analysis and extended clinical supervision. Dr. Jung continues, "The psychotherapist, however, must understand not only the patient. It is equally important that he should understand himself. For that reason the *sine qua non* is the analysis of the analyst, what is called the training analysis. The patient's treatment begins with the doctor, so to speak. Only if the doctor knows how to cope with himself and his own problems will he be able to teach the patient to do the same. Only then. In the training analysis, the doctor must learn to know his own psyche and to take it seriously…"

Physicians and other practitioners, as well as analysts, should have the kind of personal development included in their training that makes them able to deal with human suffering personally and to know themselves well enough to have become seasoned in their knowledge of how tough life is. We cannot be perfectly trained in these areas, but we must be aware of, and be in the process of, our own development to have a positive healing effect on the people we are trying to help. Of course, our one-sided training perspectives in allopathic medicine almost ignore the importance of this kind of healing work. In medicine, only a few residency programs seem to have basic courses in how to relate to patients, and currently these courses are not receiving much support. That is one of the most important reasons for this book, which is meant to help you develop this healing approach for yourself. It is crucially important, both in support of our treatments and our healing, to be able to ask ourselves, **"What can I do for myself?"** and **then do it**.

The current educational system for medical doctors, psychologists, and other therapists, unfortunately, is based primarily on the accumulation of knowledge as facts and data and then on applying this knowledge and information rationally and systematically. As a result of this one-sided model, when the body-mind-spirit questions come up, as they have been doing for some time now, our educational systems do not know how to get into an appropriate paradigm to even be able to ask intelligent questions about the interrelatedness of these aspects of ourselves. In this book, we are honoring the Hippocratic method and opening ourselves to the knowledge of the Asklepion approach as it is brought up to date through Jungian psychology.

Thoughts and Questions to Ponder...

As mentioned...one of the most important reasons for this book is to help you develop this healing approach for yourself.

It is crucially important to be in support of our treatments and our healing process and to ask ourselves,

"What can I do for myself?"

What are ways that you can participate in your own healing journey?

Are there moments when you are aware that you are listening in a deeper way?

How can you incorporate this practice of listening into your daily life?

How do I feel when I say each of these sentences?

I am choosing to be my whole self.

I am choosing to live my full self.

Life is calling me to heal, to grow, to be my whole self.

*I choose to become who I am meant to be,
to live my most authentic self.*

I choose to emerge from my old shell.

*I choose to grow beyond the restricted boundaries
that do not serve my full self.*

Do I feel that in a way I am already listening to my big Self?

Other thoughts...

CHAPTER 6

The Journey into Sacred Space

When the reverberations of shock subside in you,
May grace come to restore you to balance.
May it shape a new space in your heart
To embrace this illness as a teacher
Who has come to open your life to new worlds.

— JOHN O'DONOHUE

Now let's see how the Asklepion approach to healing, as updated through Jungian psychology, began to work for Beth as it had worked for me for decades. A few months after she had been working with me, Beth wanted to take a session to sum up where we had been and what she had thought along the way. She began by telling me, "When you first began to suggest that I might want to do some journaling and write down my dreams, I thought, 'Oh, darn! More work to do, and I'm too tired and feel down too often to want

Figure 11. Carl Jung

to take on another task.' Then, after a particularly bad week, I had a dream that was so beautiful that I had to write it down." Beth went on to share, "I dreamed that I was in this beautiful, elegant garden. It was full of flowers and benches. As I sat on a marble bench, I saw a stream flowing into a pond filled with lovely fish. As I looked around, there was a stone wall, like part of an ancient temple. In the wall, in specially cut-out places, were a silver-handled sword in a scabbard and a golden chalice. When I looked around, there was a stunning woman standing behind me. She had silver hair and was putting a hand on my shoulder.

She seemed like a goddess or an angel. Then I woke up with a feeling of peace like I hadn't felt since before my diagnosis."

Figure 12. Hidden Hands

As Beth spoke, I was thinking that she had made a step forward. She was accepting her reality, and our work had opened a small door that allowed her unconscious to speak to her, and she heard it through a healing dream. She was experiencing the inner support that can come to us. Then Beth continued, "The garden reminded me of what you said about needing a sacred space for healing. This must be my sacred space inside of me. Then I thought, 'I need a sacred space outside too.' I decided to set up a corner in my study with a candle and a few images that are special to me. When I feel like it, this is where I will reflect, pray, journal, or do whatever I feel I have the strength to do. I decided that to set the mood when I sit down at this table, I will close my eyes and take three deep breaths, inhaling and exhaling slowly, like I once was taught to do in a workshop."

Now Beth is finding her own way to follow the old tradition of going to a temple of Asclepius. She realizes that in today's world she has to create a sacred space for herself. Fortunately, a dream opened the door for her. Beth then added, "I think that I am learning that you are right, and I can't use determination to drive this work. The garden is telling me I have to relax into it, to cultivate it." What Beth is discovering here is vitally important. We know that by the time children are in a standard kindergarten for six weeks, they have internalized that what the teacher tells them to do is work, and what they want to do is play. After that, we separate things into tasks and play, and deep down we resent new tasks being thrust into our already busy or tiring or exhausting days. Too many tasks to face, like too many battles to fight, leave us feeling fatigued, resentful, and discouraged.

So our inner journey of healing, dreams, journaling, imagination, transformation, visualizations, and so on must become sacred rituals. They are neither work nor play, though sometimes they're demanding, and sometimes they are fun. As I do them, I am moved by my love of growth and transformation, of becoming more fully human, and of eventually discovering my deep gratitude for life in the midst of my suffering…and then even finding moments of joy.

◆ ◆ ◆

As is evident, Beth is starting to move in this direction of growth and transformation. When our dialog continued, I asked Beth more about the dream. She shared, "I think the sword in the dream means that sometimes I must be able to be fierce and creative in giving time to myself—time to be in my sacred space. The chalice, I think, means there is a source for the water of life in me, no matter how bad I'm feeling." I wanted to cheer, and I did give a huge smile and said, "Bravo!" Beth is truly opening to the depths within herself.

I would add that the sword is also a symbol of discrimination as well as power. It is important to know how to listen. For example, when my soul says, "OK, Bud, that's enough for now. Digest this, rest, and then come back," I need to listen. I must remember that I come to this sacred place with love and devotion and a desire to be open to life and my deeper Self, and it is alright to just come to this place for rest and to find peace.

If I can't come this way, I may actually need to be writing in my Darkness Journal to explore why. We all have to remind ourselves that there must also be room for our grief, anger, discouragement, and bitterness. The room for that expression is in our Darkness Journal, and it, too, should have a place in our sacred space.

A few weeks later, I ushered Beth into my office after she had undergone a series of tests at her doctor's that left her feeling anxious and terrified about how her MS was affecting her cognitive abilities. After listening to her carefully and getting a real sense of what it felt like to be in her shoes, I shared some of my experiences with visualizations. I recounted how, for a number of nights after my cancer surgery, I spent time visualizing myself as the prodigal son coming home to that strong, loving father figure in Rembrandt's painting. These visualizations helped me feel safe, secure that I was returning home and that I was being greeted with the support for a new life. I suggested to Beth that she develop a series of visualizations in which she returned in her imagination to the garden in her dream when she needed peace and also to find an inner center that she would trust. I encouraged her to include the numinous woman who had given her such a loving, healing touch, and I also suggested that she remember that the chalice and the sword were available to her.

Movies, stories, dreams, fantasies, longing for hugs, and many things teach us that what we imagine, we also experience. The Jungian analyst Guy Corneau says in his work with his own cancer, "Visualization works because the brain doesn't distinguish between imaginary states and real facts. We get ulcers from worrying about money whether the concern is real or imagined. Reality begins in the imagination... What is real for the brain is our inner state." Our imaginations affect our immune system, our strengths, vitality, and hope. So we need to cultivate our imagination and join actively with it, allowing it to help us create an environment of healing and wholeness within ourselves. The ancient journey to the temple of Asclepius was the beginning of a journey toward opening to our unconscious and imagination.

Figure 13. The Return of the Prodigal Son by Rembrandt

As Beth and I moved forward with her inner work and journey of healing, I encouraged her to begin a written dialog with the woman or angel in her dream. I suggested that she talk with her as an intimate friend and a wisdom figure. She could share her thoughts and feelings with her and ask her help for whatever she wanted help with.

I will talk more about dialoging later, and I also recommend chapter 6, "Dialoguing as Interrelating," in my book *Sacred Selfishness*. Such dialoging is part of what is called Active Imagination in Jungian work. Active Imagination gives both form and voice to parts of our personality, bodies, and illnesses that normally aren't heard. It sets up lines of communication with them. It means actively experiencing ourselves in writing in order to help us differentiate from this particular part of ourselves and then to begin "actively" listening to what this part of our self replies. We must learn to listen in a way that seeks to understand these parts of ourselves. We are not trying to get them to go away, to shut up, or to leave us alone. We don't attack them unless they attack us. If they do, which is rare, we need to take them quickly to a good Jungian analyst or therapist. In fact, a good Jungian analyst who is trained in and has been through the "Asklepion" process of healing can be very helpful in this kind of work.

Through our dialogs, we learn to listen to these features in ourselves, to understand the parts they play in our lives, and to see how they are challenging us to help an old way of life and an old way of perceiving life to die so a new one can be born. Now I must admit that Active Imagination was the hardest thing for me to grasp in Jungian psychology. I have a strong ego, and it likes to be in charge. It took me quite a while to become open to the process, even though I had always thought I was open to imagination. But the results that I now get are priceless. When I began, I had all of the typical defenses: I didn't have time; I felt stupid; I thought I was making it all up; I knew I was making it up; it was silly…all that kind of stuff. Initially, it helped me to imagine I was a playwright, and I simply wrote until the voices of the "characters" became their own.

As Beth developed her skills at dialoging, we took the process two steps further. I invited Beth to dialog with her illness, her MS, and with the lesions forming in her body. When I did my own illness dialogs, I found beginning the process difficult and scary. So I asked Beth to imagine the figure of the divine or wise woman from her dream standing there beside her with her hand upon her shoulder, giving her support and protection. It is often very helpful to call on our unconscious to send us its support through the image of an angel, a divine being, or a wisdom figure in the temple of our imagination during these situations. Then I suggested that she listen to her illness and let it express its thoughts, memories, feelings about her current and former life, and her bodily sensations, and even note colors that came up. Then she was to do the same thing with her lesions. She understood that it is a major effort to listen to her body—to see it symbolically and metaphorically, and to see there is a purpose and consciousness available to us through it. She can also ask her body, her lesions, and her illness what would help them heal. She may also go a step further and visualize her body glowing with warmth and health and giving comfort and healing, even love, to her lesions.

Writing these lines reminded me of two of my favorite quotations from the wise and loving poet Rainer Maria Rilke. The first one is, "If we arrange our life according to that principle which counsels us that we must always hold to the difficult, then that, which now still seems to us the most alien, will become what we most trust and find most faithful." The second quotation, which follows this one beautifully, is, "Perhaps the dragons of our lives are princesses who are only waiting to see us once, beautiful, and brave. Perhaps everything terrible is in its deepest being something that needs our love."

From the standpoint of the symbolic life, as Jung conceptualized it, our symptoms and illnesses often have the function of translating the images from our deeper Self—which may be having trouble manifesting itself through the noise of our busyness and the cage we set up in our need to control our lives. Perhaps they are challenging us to new love and meaning.

Beth understands the radical perspective that her lesions may be acting out as the representative of the wholeness of life. She also understands that she is activating the right side of her brain, the connection to the "Master," who should be the ruler of how we experience life and how we live and connect to the Self, the life force, and its direction within us. She is also inviting them to heal as she heeds their messages. I do believe that as our illnesses offer us more directions, we may also offer them new directions, such as to heal or leave. The Jungian analyst Guy Corneau suggested to his cancer cells that once he had fulfilled the tasks they asked of him, they were no longer needed. And after his long and intense inner work (he reported that he dialoged with them daily for over two years, as mentioned), they went into remission. In my own case, my cancer did not heal, but my dialog with it revolutionized my life, as I will share later.

The symbolic life opened by Asklepion Healing and Jungian psychology is crucially important. The symbolic life that is the life of the imagination is filled with the language of poetry and religion, symbols and metaphors. These affect us. They activate a wide array of brain circuits. When we compromise this process, we compromise our healing capacities. Hippocratic medicine tends to concretize symbols and metaphors. This process then causes us to dismiss the symbols and metaphors as meaningless and prompts us to cut ourselves off from our archetypal depths and the healing potentials within us.

Beth soon discovered that active imagination produced a radical shift in her experience of her illness. Through this work that is ongoing for her, she moved away from old patterns and toward the healing aspects of living more authentically. What Beth has learned is that radical hope is born through the inner journey as we develop confidence in life and our own depth's ability to support us. She also understands that body, mind, spirit, conscious, and unconscious are all parts of the same whole. The big Self acts like the hub of a wheel, centering and channeling our life force, arranging our potentials, and fostering their development like the carefully spaced spokes that reach out from the hub to the rim of a wheel. The rim acts like our personality, supporting our progress and movement through life, yet its support rests on the center, the Self. When we are in touch with the Self's support, we will discover radical hope and its expectation for the future, and we will experience a fundamental sense of peace.

Thoughts and Questions to Ponder...

This may now be the time to create sacred space inside yourself in order to reflect, pray, journal, or do whatever you feel you have the strength to do.

You may want to first close your eyes and then take three deep breaths...inhaling and exhaling very slowly...before you begin journaling.

Here are some journaling suggestions:

As you begin to take the opportunity to return to your true Self, what does that feel like? What emotions does that opportunity bring up for you?

Take time to dialog...to have a conversation with your big Self.

Sometime this week, put your journal beside your bed, and in the morning, take time to write down any of your dreams, if you remember them.

Here are some quotes to reflect on:

"We have suffered a radical shock, and we are seeking radical hope and a radically new life."

The origins of the word "radical" mean having roots below the surface, reaching deep into the earth in a way that is fundamental to life and vital to the soul.

What supportive roots do you experience below your surface?

Even in my darkest moments, I breathe in and I breathe out and I let my self be still at the very center of my center.

How do I feel when I do that?

In my darkest moments, I am beginning to allow myself to receive strength in order to be present to my small self and be receptive to my deepest Self.

Share some of your thoughts.

"Healing isn't about staying alive...It is about what we are, how we live, and moving closer to our essence and our wholeness."

What do you think about this quotation?

Does it resonate with you?

"Whether we are clinically ill or not, life is calling us to healing, growth, and wholeness—to become who we are meant to be, to live our most authentic selves, to grow beyond our boundaries to own our truest potentials, and to become strong enough to give love, compassion, and acceptance to our greatest struggles— and to find meaning in our darkest moments so that new life and creativity can emerge from them."

What do you think about this quotation?

Other thoughts...

CHAPTER 7

Response to Pain:
The Measure of the Human Spirit

As short as the time
From spark to flame
So brief may the distance be
Between heart and being.

— JOHN O'DONOHUE

I want to continue our exploration by talking about meaning and the human spirit, which are cornerstones in my life and in every kind of true healing. Often we make the shallow and all too human mistake of believing that a "good life" or a "life of abundance" is the way the Divine wants us to live. However, life teaches us otherwise… it teaches us that the power of human vulnerability can inspire our greatest expressions of love, understanding, and compassion, and can bring transformation. Crises and illnesses force us to ask ourselves, "What approach to life leads us to misery and self-destruction?" and "What approach to life makes us the most human, the most truthful with ourselves, and leads us to touch the Divine?" These are the questions that haunt and energize our long, painful drama of searching for Self-knowledge if we fully engage in our lives. They are also the questions that can open the doors to moments of profound gratitude and joy, to our wholeness.

Healing moments in our lives are when we are moving closer to our wholeness and we feel it. Beth felt it when the woman in her dream placed her hand upon her shoulder. Our authentic identity becomes the touchstone for our healing, and we become bigger people, larger than we were before. There is a pattern for our life's expression of our potentials within our Self, a greater dream than we know, and healing helps us move closer to that dream whether we are sick or well. The wholeness to which that healing leads is far beyond the perfection we have been taught that we should be seeking.

As the "Master" is returned to our lives, and when our left and right brain work in harmony, we begin to access our deeper Self and feel its guidance and support. The vehicle of our right brain and much of our deeper Self is symbolized by what we often think of as "the heart." Our symbolic heart is an organ of vision, a way of seeing that can help our intellect to look below the surface of things. There we can see the meaning in the events in our lives and be strengthened by them. Our ability to see this meaning in our lives and their events transforms our experience, strengthens us, energizes our commitments, and increases our satisfaction. We use our expertise and technology along with our knowledge in our efforts to cure ourselves and others. Yet it is the Asklepion approach—the approach into depths of who we are and the visions of the heart—that brings healing. I would like to share with you a true story that illustrates what I mean.

One of the greatest analysts that those of us in my generation of analysts in training in Zurich knew was Dr. Sonja Marjiash. She had a progressive and crippling spinal disease, and it took her hours to get up every morning. Then, wheelchair bound and in pain, she spent a few hours every afternoon healing others and changing lives. Sonja told us that she assigned a musical note to each level of her pain, and together the notes became music in her imagination and transformed her pain into a melody. Dr. Marjiash had also discovered the difference between our technological approach to pain management, which couldn't bring her total relief, and the path of our deeper Self to managing her suffering and living the vision of her heart in order to bring healing to others. Dr. Jung himself continued to work and wrote his greatest books after his major heart attack and while continuing to suffer from congestive heart failure. Our response to pain and death is often the greatest measure of how precious we know life to be, and it is also a measure of the human spirit because we make it a measure of our spirit.

One of the most difficult issues I have had to come to grips with is how to deal with people who can't be cured. Dr. Marjiash was a living example of how the inner journey can still support us and bring love, healing, joy, and wholeness into our lives. Both she and Dr. Jung had a great sense of humor. The quest for healing and wholeness and becoming grounded in our Self can help us find a good life, even though it is not an easy life...even if we are dying. In his final moments of life, the physician and writer Oliver Sacks shared with us in his book *Gratitude* how his journey led him to face death with a profound sense of gratitude for life. I have heard many such stories.

Frequently, when I am talking about the healing power of illness, someone will ask me if I believe that illness can be a gift. My answer is no. I believe that our gift is in the innermost heart of each of us where it interacts with the Divine. I have called this part of ourselves the Self. In it—if we can reach it, and most of this book is devoted to doing that—we will discover our deepest capacities for resilience. In this holy ground dwells our ability to search for meaning, new life, more wholeness, and more love in the midst of our despair, pain, and suffering. For me, illness is no gift, even though it has shaped my destiny throughout my life. But our *capacity to respond* to illness and our suffering in the ways I am presenting in this book *is* a great gift.

All too often we think of heroism as winning, conquering, defeating, overcoming all odds, and having a positive attitude. And as we pursue this course, we invariably fall into our subtle addiction to perfection even in our spiritual pursuits. But when midlife, aging, trauma, or illness throw us into the search for meaning that activates a radical shift in life, we need to find the support of our own depths and the Divine within us—the Self with a capital *S*. This journey back into our full humanity calls for a new kind of heroism. This heroism is to face our fate and say yes to it...to what is already happening to us...to dive into it and into own our depths.

This is the turn that Parsifal made when he turned from being a glorious knight of King Arthur's Round Table, the fulfillment of a childhood dream, into a knight seeking the Holy Grail. Parsifal was willing to ask the right questions of the Grail in order to bring new life and wholeness into the wasteland—the symbol of our inner state. It is the turn that Chiron the centaur made in Greek mythology when he gave up eternal life and the inflated sense that he could be his own redeemer. After that, Chiron chose to cooperate with the forces that shaped him and at that moment was transformed from a tragic victim into a courageous seeker, one who was prepared to plunge into the unknown search for healing, wholeness, authenticity, and a new dynamic spirit of life. By doing this, he became the guiding archetypal spirit of the wounded healer. When we are in pain—whether it is psychological, emotional, or physical—by making this turn toward the hero or heroine's quest, this choice lessens the pain. This is a key component of the healing process, which we will explore later in this book.

Drinking from the chalice of Destiny means facing my fate and calling on my deeper Self for support. Doing this lifts me out of the victimhood of an unconscious fate and sets me on the classic hero's quest that Dr. Carl Jung and the mythologist Joseph Campbell spoke so much about. It gives radical rebirth—transformation—to anyone who chooses this path and gives him or her the possibility of helping to renew and transform our culture. This whole journey that I am presenting is directed toward our finding meaning and individuation through our illnesses. It is choosing the path of being a seeker. It is a radical perspective which brings radical hope as we learn to understand that individuation itself is a radical series of transformations. As we realize that initiation is the rite of dying to an old life and being born into a new one, we see that illness, as an initiation, initiates us continually into knowing what it means to become more fully human. And becoming more fully human initiates us into becoming truly spiritual. The classic hero or heroine's quest always results in bringing new values back to the culture. So the next question is, "How can we bring new values from our illness to our culture?" Here is how we can do it:

If we live our illness with support from our Self or our depths, and humbly;

If we become open to carrying our suffering and fear openly but with grace, after accepting the full presence of them;

If we become open to letting others fully express their caring for us, and if we are willing to be "trouble" in their lives;

If we are willing to be seen in our vulnerability and in our humiliations;

If we stand unashamedly for life until we know deep inside that it is time for us to accept our death.

What I am saying is that if we open ourselves to receive love, care, and compassion, and are willing to be dependent on others, we offer them the gift of discovering their best capacities as human beings. We then become significant participants in the redemption of our culture. We are also helping to loosen the stranglehold our culture has on us that tells us to always be positive, productive, busy, and self-critical. We can help our culture to learn what it means to be truly human, to place compassion above productivity, community above individualism, and love above busyness, and to learn that our quest for the Divine is a quest to become fully human.

Then we have learned why all of our great religions so conspicuously value suffering, and we can see that our suffering...our illness... has a meaning and a profound role to play in teaching our world how to cherish the greatest values life has to offer. This has been a heartbreakingly difficult journey for me. Yet it has also brought great moments of love and joy...and the journey continues. I hope that what I am learning will also make your life richer and more hopeful.

Thoughts and Questions to Ponder...

Taking time to explore my soul-pain...

What is my soul-pain about?

What does my soul-pain feel like?

*Are there feelings within me that I have not yet acknowledged...
noticed...felt...accepted...worked with...healed?*

Do I have feelings of being an outcast?

Do I have feelings of not being in control?

Take time to answer these questions. You don't need to answer
them all at once... Breathe in and breathe out and consider
them... You may answer them a step at a time...

Have I feelings of shame?
Describe any feelings you are experiencing about this.

Have I feelings of blame?
Describe any feelings you are experiencing about this.

Have I feelings of anger?
Describe any feelings you are experiencing about this.

Have I feelings of sorrow?
Describe any feelings you are experiencing about this.

Have I feelings of grief?
Describe any feelings you are experiencing about this.

Have I feelings of failure?
Describe any feelings you are experiencing about this.

Have I feelings of being judged? Of being criticized?

Do I have feelings that this illness is my fault?

Have I been blaming myself?

Do I have feelings of being unworthy?

What are my reflections about meaning and the human spirit?

*How can I let them be cornerstones in my life
and in my true healing?*

*How might some of my habits be getting in the way
of my true self coming forth?*

Other thoughts...

CHAPTER 8

Reclaiming and Revitalizing Our Unlived Lives

May the fragile harvesting of this slow light
Help to release whatever has become false in you.
May you trust this light to clear a path
Through all the fog of old unease and anxiety
Until you feel arising within you a tranquility
Profound enough to call the storm to stillness.

— JOHN O'DONOHUE

"What is my unlived life...and where did it come from?" is a question that I am often asked. My answer is to respond by saying to imagine that your life is threatened, and in order to escape the threat, you must create another identity, a false cover. In a way, this is what we all do, beginning in our earliest years and continuing as we grow up and seek to fit into the world. Before too many years have passed, we start to think this false cover is who we really are.

But in reality, there is much more inside of us than we included in our disguise, and these parts of us will eventually begin crying out to be recognized, to be accepted, and to become a living part of who we are. If we keep them repressed, locked away deep inside, they can become stormy forces, turbulent moods, and can even make us sick. We call these cut-off and rejected aspects of ourselves our *shadow*. Our shadow also wants to participate in determining our future and to help us let go of characteristics in our identity that we have identified with too rigidly.

Our unlived lives take their revenge through our restless feelings of dissatisfaction, through our guilt over failing to live up to our hopes and dreams, through our emotional pain that undermines us, through our destructive habits, and especially through our illnesses. The roots of the things that often disrupt our lives, drain our energy, and thwart our intentions lie in the conflict around our longings for growth and freedom, our longings for remaining in the peace and safety of our old selves, and our reluctance or refusal to pay the price for our authenticity through the special kind of suffering that comes through transforming ourselves, our shadows.

In his great poem "The Age of Anxiety," W. H. Auden recounts, "We would rather be ruined than changed. We would rather die in our dread than climb the cross of the moment and let our illusions die." This special kind of suffering I am talking about comes when we try our best to acknowledge the hidden forces that drive our lives, to seek to transform them, and to live the unlived portions of our lives that have been left in their wake. This venture quickly teaches us that to love life and to be fully engaged in it will threaten the walls supporting the identity we have so carefully constructed.

Most of us grew up wanting to define ourselves as some version of a person that aims to think positively; be nice, good, and caring; to handle money well; to take obligations seriously; and in general to act responsibly. In fact, to even begin questioning how we have defined ourselves and to begin seeking to become more conscious of our wholeness creates a fear that we may be only dimly aware of but that is as strong as our fear of death. In addition, far too many of us feel so overwhelmed by our obligations and the pace of our lives that we can only long for peace and balance rather than begin questioning. Dr. Jung's statement that he "could not imagine a fate more awful, a fate worse than death, than a life lived in perfect balance and harmony" is baffling and scary to anyone that is already overwhelmed by their lives.

The creation story of our unlived lives starts soon after we are born and we begin shaping ourselves to avoid shame, punishment, harm, and embarrassment, as well as to gain approval and encouragement. Little daily decisions and bargains with ourselves help us become collaborators in the demise of our spirit. Choosing how we will be good, what we will rebel against, how desirable certain playmates are, whether to accept bribes for grades, or whether to pursue good grades in order to "earn" love all help us "sell out" our integrity and undermine our self-worth. Making compromises, and embracing practicality, being sensible, the promise of a "good life" with success, and the avoidance of pain, keep us off the byways that could add depth, meaning, and vitality to our lives. The inner voices of our integrity, conscience, and authenticity weaken against the pressure of conventional wisdom, busy and demanding lives, and the fearful appearance of the world. Before long, we are so embedded in our identities that, without knowing it, what we have considered our best characteristics may have become expressions of our major compromises. Yet questioning ourselves has become difficult and threatening, as we fear that it may disrupt our lives.

I remember working with Janice, who was brought up as the youngest of four children with a cold mother and an angry father. She survived her childhood by doing well in school and later by pleasing her superiors. But in midlife, her denied needs and potentials rebelled, leaving her overweight and depressed. The answer for her was not in the mainstream treatment of her depression. It was in getting to know the negative wounds that kept her so self-critical and self-belittling that an important part of her continued to be paralyzed in passivity. Working through these wounds freed her inner strength that could then support her to have her own voice. Psychologically, it was like Cinderella breaking free to meet her prince. This prince helped her recognize her denied capacities and gave her the strength to devote her life to bringing these abilities into her living reality. I also recall John, a middle-aged man who had been raised to be a pleaser, to repress the strength of his own desires, and to sublimate his needs into finding approval by satisfying others. But after two failed marriages, he realized that his relationships had been formed on a lie, a version of himself that wasn't deeply real, and on an idealism that would make any relationship hopeless. To begin with, he had to find the courage to face disapproval, to take the risks of first standing up to the voices of his indoctrination in his psyche, and then to confront the people his new identity disturbed. This group also included the people he had unconsciously trained to expect him to be a pleaser. Then, in order to free his anima, to allow his inner Cinderella, or feeling self, to come to the ball, he had to explore his moods—the ones he had tried to conceal, even from himself, along with the blocked emotions they represented.

In these two oversimplified examples, both people had to face the fear and loneliness that had pressured them into their roles and then to face their anger and grief over their early reality. This vital work released new, potent energy within them and increased their feelings of strength, competence, and hope in the future. Our unlived lives—the values, visions, talents, and longings we haven't admitted—are actually necessary to develop as part of our wholeness and are essential in supporting our true purpose, meaning, and trust in life. The unlived life will begin rebelling when its repression becomes a toxic part of our makeup, and when our failure to love ourselves is also failing our future. This rebellion will test us in the halls of the most sacrosanct and vulnerable parts of how we value ourselves, in the foundations of our identity, and in the ways we are afraid of what other people will think about us. Facing ourselves and our unlived lives isn't easy work. We call it "confronting our shadow." Yet the need for it shows that we are being called by the life force within our depths, the Self, to become our own true self…to truly experience a second birth…to become a cocreator with the Divine and to live beyond our conventional ideas of the "good life" in order to help heal and redeem ourselves and our part of the world.

Our greatest spiritual traditions are based on the themes of self-knowledge, growth, and transformation. The mystical traditions raise our journey into wholeness…to a journey into holiness. This lifts our lives into a realm that is far more profound than simply trying to be good and happy. The call of our unlived life is a call from our Self. The Self, in Jungian terms, represents our inherent drive for consciousness and wholeness. Archetypally, it is the supreme ordering system in our psyche and is continually focused on getting us to develop and fulfill the highest potentials within us. The real struggle is between our willingness to participate in our transformation and our often-unconscious yearning to stay safely grounded in our old selves.

The failure to search and listen for the calls of the Self in the midst of my struggles or to avoid the encounters that reveal them is a risk I am no longer willing to take. I have learned very clearly that my illnesses, though perhaps caused by many factors, are also telling me there is a split with myself that needs to be faced and healed.

Thoughts and Questions to Ponder...

Our greatest spiritual traditions are based on the themes of self-knowledge, growth, and transformation. These traditions raise our journey into wholeness...to a journey into holiness. This lifts our lives into a realm that is far more profound than simply trying to be good and happy. The call of our unlived life is a call from our Self.

What are my reflections about this?

Reflect upon these statements, and write about them:

> *I am willing to recognize the conditions of my life.*
>
> *I am willing to experience the bitterness and the pain.*
>
> *I am willing to allow for the deep sweetness of life to reveal itself to me.*
>
> *My shadow is that part of me and my own energy which I hide or repress.*

(We usually think of our shadow as being our darker side, yet often it also contains much of our positive potential as well.)

> *I am beginning to recognize my shadow.*

Consider what parts of yourself you have hidden or repressed... Write about them.

Our projections are evident when we see in someone else some feature of ourselves that we've disowned. We usually consider our projections as being an aspect of our darker side; however, often they may contain much of our positive potentials as well.

> *I am beginning to recognize my projections.*

Consider what parts of yourself you have "disowned"... Write about them.

Other thoughts...

CHAPTER 9

Searching for Meaning

May you learn to use this illness
As a lantern to illuminate
The new qualities that will emerge in you.

– JOHN O'DONOHUE

As a boy, I grew up in a childhood traumatized by cancer and death. As I was struggling in young adulthood to break out of the shroud of darkness that had enfolded me during those early years, I read the great psychoanalyst Viktor Frankl's book *Man's Search for Meaning*. Dr. Frankl and his pregnant wife, father, mother, and brother were put in Nazi death camps during World War II, and all of his dear ones perished in these camps, while he survived. While in these camps, Dr. Frankl also experienced extreme starvation and terrible illnesses.

From his experience in these camps, Dr. Frankl concluded that ***survival depends upon being oriented toward the future and toward a meaning to be fulfilled by our life in the future***. He also concluded that even if we can't survive, that orientation supports our meeting death with heads held high. He went on to say that "we must never forget that we may also find meaning in life even when confronted with a hopeless situation as its helpless victim when facing a fate that cannot be changed. For what then counts and matters is to bear witness to the uniquely human potential at its best, which is to turn one's predicament into a human achievement…we are challenged to change ourselves." And he concludes, "Suffering can have meaning if it changes us for the better." At the time I read these words, I was in my early twenties, and I wondered, How did he do that? How did he figure this out in a concentration camp? What made him different from those other inmates? And I also wondered, How can I do that?

Then, a few years ago, I read an article in our local newspaper by Tom Swift, a man who was virtually helpless with ALS (amyotrophic lateral sclerosis, Lou Gehrig's disease). In his article, Tom shared that for the past five years, he has been preparing to die. Now, he states, "I have had a change in plans. I have decided to prepare to live." He explains there is a difference between "accepting my death and being resigned to it. ALS may kill me, but not because I have given up hope." He then remarked that he will continue to be full of hope, faith, and love. I was deeply moved reading his words, and once again I wondered, How did this person get to this place of radical hope?

◆ ◆ ◆

As I am writing, I am reminded of the words I wrote in chapter 7 about the measure of the human spirit. I said that I don't believe that illness is a gift. I wrote these words with the full knowledge that illness has shaped my destiny, who I am, and my major experiences of life. I believe our true gift is in the innermost heart of each of us, the big Self that intersects with the Divine. In this deepest part of ourselves, if we can reach it—and I am devoting this book to being a guide for that journey—we will discover our most profound capacities for resilience, purpose, and meaning, as well as new life, more wholeness, and more love in the midst of our despair, pain, and suffering. It was from this ground that the mystical visions arose in Viktor Frankl that changed and transformed his life while he was starving to death, emaciated and ill in the death camp. Illness is no gift, but our capacity to respond to the illness and our suffering in the ways I'm presenting in this book *is* a great gift.

This gift can go even further. The mystical visions that came to Dr. Frankl brought with them a revelation of how to transcend his situation and a compelling call—like a Divine decree—to expand himself and to bring the results of his experience into the world. At this moment, the big Self, or the Divine within, had called him to a vocation that gave purpose and meaning to his terrible experiences and a direction for the rest of his life.

The same was true of Tom Swift. As he lay dying a slow, terrible death, he was called to a new vocation, one of purpose and, I pray, one that gave him a sense of peace as well as meaning. His series of articles moved and inspired everyone in our community that I know. Reading one of his articles instantly brought us into the depths of what it means to be truly human. I cannot even begin to imagine the hope and comfort these articles brought to our suffering friends in this community. Can you imagine finding a vocation in our process of dying? It took me a long time to let the realization of such a potential into my heart. Over the past twelve years, I have watched my daughter and her family live in the shadow of her progressive multiple sclerosis. Through this whole process, I believe they have had their own visions, and they have found what the spiritual writer C. S. Lewis would describe as glory. In his book *The Weight of Glory*, Lewis says that we desire too little out of the lives we have. He writes that we smother the inner voice that could carry us beyond ourselves and our circumstances. He challenges us to become luminous and "to become a kind of living electric light bulb." I have watched this happen to my daughter and her family in the community they have attracted, inspired, and energized. They have found a spirit of love, courage, and community. They are luminous in their own way, as Viktor Frankl and Tom Swift were in their ways. I am also sad because I see that as long as the emissary rules in our culture, they suffer more, and needlessly. Their suffering is heartbreakingly multiplied by the impossible expenses of medical care, and the resulting stress bleeds them of energy and hope.

I learned all those decades ago from Viktor Frankl that we have a choice about how we can respond to life. And in difficult circumstances, we can make the choice to discover new meaning in our lives when all seems lost in darkness. Taking to heart the words of Viktor Frankl and then becoming a Jungian analyst, I have learned a way to get to this place of purpose and meaning that opens to the fullness of life, that facilitates our medical treatment, and that sometimes brings a cure and helps us realize that healing isn't about staying alive—it is about what we are, how we live, and moving closer to our essence and our wholeness.

How to get there—that is the journey I want to share with you in the rest of this book and that I want to involve you in. At its deepest level, it is the same journey for all of us. It is a path that our nature is asking us to take in response to the questions that life is asking of each of us...of discovering and fulfilling the meaning that our unique life is offering. Whether we are clinically ill or not, the golden need in human life is still calling us...to healing, growth, and wholeness...to becoming who we are meant to be, to living our most authentic selves, to growing beyond our boundaries, to owning our truest potentials, and to being strong enough to give love, compassion, and acceptance to our greatest struggles. It is also to finding meaning in our darkest moments so that new life and creativity can emerge from them.

When we consider this journey through the eyes of Viktor Frankl, Tom Swift, or Dr. Carl Jung, we see that radical hope is very different from the conventional hope that is so often offered by the shallow optimism of our culture. Our culture focuses on defeating illnesses, overcoming our so-called weaknesses, promoting illusions of cures, and promises of easy answers while avoiding the real depth of life's challenges to our entire being.

This journey of meaning is one of discovering the true purpose of being spiritual, and it teaches us that being spiritual results from our becoming fully human.

Thoughts and Questions to Ponder...

"I learned all those decades ago from Viktor Frankl that we have a choice about how we can respond to life. And in difficult circumstances, we can make the choice to discover new meaning in our lives when all seems lost in darkness."

What are your thoughts about this?

In your difficult circumstances, can you make the choice to discover new meaning in your life?

What choices are you considering in terms of responding to life?

Our culture focuses on defeating illnesses, overcoming our so-called weaknesses, providing illusions of cures, and promises of easy answers while avoiding the real depth of life's challenges to our entire being.

This journey is the real purpose of being spiritual, and it teaches us that being spiritual results from our becoming fully human.

What are your thoughts about this?

Other thoughts...

CHAPTER 10

Trusting the Process in the Quest for Life

May you find in yourself
A courageous hospitality
Toward what is difficult,
Painful, and unknown.

— John O'Donohue

Every major passage or event in our lives calls for a reorientation of who we are and how we are going to relate to the world. We may describe this change in ourselves as an initiation—a leaving of our old selves in order to allow for a new and hopefully larger, more open, and renewed self to emerge. In Jungian psychology, we call this period of change a period of transformation. The well-known mythologist Joseph Campbell defined this path of human development as the hero's or heroine's journey. We use this centuries-old classic mythological term hero or heroine in the sense of facing our own lives as a journey that requires courage and stamina to grow and transform ourselves.

In far too many cases, our inclination is to turn our back on our creative choices and to retreat into defensive, narrow positions. There we try to keep what we can of our old selves and continue to live by our old illusions of practicality and conventional wisdom as a defense against our fear of risk and change. The journey of transformation doesn't happen overnight, but we do know something about this sacred path…I have traveled it many times. I traveled it during the time of my illness…and have also made this journey with many men and women in my practice. Knowing more about the path—how we can approach it and how we can experience it—helps us face ourselves and our futures with inspiration and hope.

As I have shared before, Dr. Jung explains the challenges and potentials in our life's journey as the *individuation process*. This process is one of growth and a movement toward becoming a whole, authentic person; it is having this inner series of transformations become expressed through how we actually live our lives.

◆ ◆ ◆

In one of our early sessions, my analysand, Beth, told me that her multiple sclerosis had sneaked into her life like a thief in the night. "I know about the reality of illness," she said. "My parents had been very ill several times, my brother had a heart attack, and friends have been sick at times. But to be honest, my thoughts, fears, and even the tears I shed quickly faded into the background. I never expected the kind of shock I experienced with my diagnosis. I've done everything medically possible that I could, and I've found that I cannot control my illness. Now I'm only hoping to slow it down. In addition, I've tried many types of alternative treatments, and while a few have helped me, more have disappointed me."

Then Beth asked me, "How can I trust this process you are speaking of? How can I believe in this path?" Now, she is asking a very legitimate question. I've actually lived this path for so long that I often take it for granted. But I know it is calling for another initiation in her life. Beth's question is real, and it caused me to stop and think. I remember when I began this journey years ago. It started when I read Jung's autobiography, *Memories, Dreams, Reflections*, for the first time, during a significant crisis in my life. I've read it may times since then, because it is a book that never fails to move my soul and to change some part of my life.

I have long since realized that the story of Jung's individuation process, of true self-realization and of coming to authentic healing and wholeness, follows a classic pattern of the archetypal hero or heroine's journey that Joseph Campbell, a student of Jung's, wrote so carefully and eloquently about. Dr. Jung puts the journey in psychological form and calls it the individuation process. Campbell puts it in mythological terms so that we can see its truth in many cultures throughout history. Both approaches show us a quest for life in its most profound sense. Both picture this journey in a way that we can understand as the Asklepion approach to healing. As you remember, this is the approach that unites body and soul. Joseph Campbell answers the question of how can we trust this approach to healing by summing up this archetypal human experience: "Furthermore, we have not to risk the adventure alone, for the heroes of all time have gone before us. The labyrinth is thoroughly known. We have only to follow the thread of the hero's path, and where we had thought to find an abomination, we shall find a god. And where we had thought to slay another, we shall slay ourselves. Where we had thought to travel outward, we will come to the center of our own existence. And where we had thought to be alone, we will be with all the world." After I had explained this aspect of the journey for a few moments, Beth interrupted me and said, "What you are telling me is that I am not alone." Yes, that's the important thing to remember: "I am not alone."

◆ ◆ ◆

In this journey, it is important to remember that one of the deepest of all patterns in the human spirit is the act of making a departure and then returning home to ourselves and life. The journey of adventure and transformation is implicit in the "between." It is a journey whose vision is elemental to our nature and, if followed, will carry us from one state of being to another. These journeys we take are journeys of becoming that call forth our most profound, powerful, and creative energies. And yet, as I have said, we are not alone in them. Our ancestors are there with us. Our great religious figures travel alongside of us. Neighbors within and without of our psyche accompany us. The great German poet Goethe reminds us that once we have committed ourselves fully, Providence moves too.

Thoughts and Questions to Ponder…

Every major passage or event in our lives calls for a reorientation of who we are and how we are going to relate to the world.

How are you reorienting in your life right now?

How is your illness an invitation to yourself to leave your old self in order to make room for a new and hopefully larger, more open, and renewed self to emerge?

How is your encounter with illness a mythic quest for life in its most profound sense? How is your encounter a hero or heroine's journey?

How is this illness an invitation to return home to yourself and to life in its truest sense?

How could it be that the journey of adventure and transformation is part of your nature and that, if followed, will carry you from one state of being to another?

How is this journey an opportunity to integrate your body, soul, and spirit?

The individuation process is one of growth and transformation… and a movement toward becoming a whole, authentic person.

How do I feel about becoming a whole, authentic person? Do I feel any resistances?

Other thoughts…

CHAPTER 11

Answering the Call for a Fulfilling Destiny

May you find the wisdom to listen to your illness.
Ask why it came. Why it chose your friendship.
Where it wants to take you. What it wants you to know.
What quality of space it wants to create in you.
What you need to learn to become more fully yourself
That your presence may shine in the world.

— JOHN O'DONOHUE

When I got my cancer diagnosis, the last thing I wanted to consider was to see this event as some kind of a *call to growth, transformation, or adventure*. I wanted to know what could be done medically, what my chances were, and what I had to go through—period. I spent a lot of time talking with doctors, gathering information, and speaking with friends who had gone through or were going through this experience. I was scared. Nothing like this had ever happened to me personally, and I treasured the closeness of my wife and family. And yet, during all of this experience, there was a part of me that knew and didn't know, that was aware and unaware—that in some way, I didn't realize I had been living against myself. There was some secret, some lurking intuition that some part of me, some part of my potentials for fulfilling who I am, had become lost. In no way did I blame myself for my cancer or for not being more aware. I know how human I am.

I also understand very well that the "call" to transformation within our lives generally comes in unpleasant ways. Illness, depression, the failure of our dreams, deaths, divorces, bankruptcies, and so on are storms on the surface of our lives that can plunge us into a world of forces that we don't understand. Professionally, in terms of the Jungian perspective, and personally as well, I see these calls as more than just wake-up calls. They are the calls that we receive to awaken to our deeper selves, to our repressed desires and conflicts, to our wounds whose effects are driving us because they need to be healed, and to our potentials that are souring inside of us because we refuse to acknowledge them and live them.

The hidden potentials we have lost and the door that can open to healing and fulfilling our lives show up in dark, ugly, terrifying forms and are frequently seen as undesirable or evil in our conventional world. In myths and fairy tales, the heralds of change appear as frogs, beasts, evil witches, dwarfs, dragons, black knights, and other sinister figures. Illness, especially cancer and illnesses like my daughter's multiple sclerosis, fit this symbolic mode completely.

A week before my surgery, I had been invited to give the C. G. Jung Memorial Lecture, sponsored by the Jung Society of Washington, DC, and to be presented at the Swiss embassy. I was especially moved because this lecture marked the fiftieth anniversary of Dr. Jung's death. My title for the lecture was "Individuation: The Promise in Jung's Legacy and Why Our Culture Has Trouble Accepting It." Developing and presenting this lecture, and the warm reception I received in Washington, were an important synchronicity in my life. Developing and presenting the lecture grounded me. It reminded me of the myth I live and of my relationship to the big Self that gives support, purpose, direction, and value to my life. It also reminded me that I was approaching a life-changing ordeal and that I would have inner support during that time.

I realized that while I needed to do everything I could to be healed, cured, and to recover, there was a second step I needed to take. I had to say yes to this experience. I had to embrace not my cancer but my journey into a new, unknown life. I had to accept that I was being initiated into a more profound level of what it means to be human and vulnerable. And finally I had to search for my capacity to expand how I was becoming and living. In other words, I realized the deeper significance and answered the call.

As I recovered from the extreme fatigue of the surgery, the tools and exercises that I have used for years and that I am sharing with you slowly came back to me. I began with guided images and progressed to journaling and dialoging for only a few minutes per day. And I let myself feel joy in the presence of my loved ones, and gratitude for my life. It is helpful for us to realize there is a pattern for this inner journey that leads us into the strength to support our difficult passages and then into an open and engaged life. I have called this journey the hero or heroine's quest, an ongoing series of initiations, and now I'm going to call it "A Journey to a Place beyond Normal."

The following map and outline represents the timeless skeleton of the journey. Each journey in actuality becomes unique when it is fleshed out by the experiences we are living, and its expression is our unique contribution to life.

KEY POINTS:

When we answer the call, we discover that it is a call to be a seeker, a call to individuation, to spiritual and psychological growth.

Individuation, our quest through self-knowledge into wholeness, always teaches us that we are more than who we think we are.

Through individuation, we learn more about suffering, love, and joy, and how difficult life can be while still being fulfilling and rewarding.

We also come to understand there are dimensions of ourselves and our potentials for realizations and self-awareness that haven't been included in our self-concept or the identity we have so carefully constructed.

Life, we discover, has the potential to be deeper and broader than we ever imagined.

Life is always empowering us to find out that how we have been living is only a fractional glimmer of what potentiality is really within us, of what generates our vitality, and of what can bring us love, wisdom, and joy.

RADICAL HOPE

We learn to live in this depth, and developing our feeling of wholeness leads us to feel at home in ourselves and in our lives. This is what life can be about.

OUTLINE

Twelve Initiatory Stages of a Journey to a Place beyond Normal

THE DEPARTURE

1. The Ordinary World
2. The Call to Adventure
3. Refusing or Answering the Call to Adventure

THE TRANSFORMATIONAL JOURNEY

4. Meeting the Supporting Power of Life
5. Crossing the First Threshold/Confronting the Threshold Guardian
6. The Road of Trials
7. Approach to the Inner Temple
8. The Turning Point

THE RETURN

9. Rewards
10. The Road Back
11. Living in Two Worlds
12. The Freedom to Live

Of course we always have a choice of becoming a seeker or, in the case of illness, of choosing denial and of identifying as a victim. Through self-discovery, we can reassess our values, reorganize our interests, recognize our more authentic selves, discover new purposes for living, and pursue more meaningful intimate relationships. Through locking ourselves into our selves, we can become further congealed within the safety of our old false selves, our adapted selves, and within the safety of our families', friends', and culture's definition of who we can or should be, and we can focus on our anger, disappointments, losses, pain, and unhappiness.

Figure 14. Map of Journey to the Sea beyond Normal

To become a seeker requires a brave, active pursuit of self-knowledge. Its rewards are that our actions and emotions become our own and turn our life into a fulfilling destiny. Then our decisions enliven us, even if they at times bring suffering, and our capacities for love and joy will surprise us. Living and finding the ultimate benefits of our journey's stages depend upon our awakening from the spell of the "good life" or "conventional wisdom" that we have been living under. Then we are able to see how this spell is also a cage that has trapped us and has limited our visions of our potentials.

To go further into this journey, we need to be devoted to re-creating ourselves and our lives by strengthening our efforts to get to know ourselves deeply, to engage fully in our lives, and to open our personalities by reflecting on our emotional responses and unconscious reactions as to how we are living.

Thoughts and Questions to Ponder...

Now, think about what I have shared with you up to this point and consider these questions:

There is a pattern for this inner journey that leads us into the strength to support our difficult passages.

How can I trust this process?

What does it mean that this pattern is archetypal, that it has been traveled throughout history?

How much do I fear devoting myself to being a seeker?

How much do I fear being fully engaged in life and reflecting on my responses to what happens to me in this life?

Please write out the kinds of thoughts and feelings that are coming up for you.

What are your feelings as you write...hope, fear, encouragement, anger, or something else?

To become a seeker requires a brave, active pursuit of self-knowledge.

Its rewards are that our actions and emotions become our own and turn our life into a fulfilling destiny.

Other thoughts...

CHAPTER 12

The Journey to a Place beyond Normal

Every time you leave home,
Another road takes you
Into a world you were never in.

         – JOHN O'DONOHUE

As we finish our discussion on trusting this path that in reality is about trusting ourselves and our responses to our experiences, let us now take a look at the stages in this journey, which I have titled "A Journey to a Place beyond Normal." These stages come under three general headings. The first heading is *The Departure*; the second is *The Transformational Journey*; and the third is *The Return*. In portraying this journey as outlined by Joseph Campbell, I explain it in terms of individuation and illness. And as we look at the specific stages, I will describe the journey as Beth and I experienced it.

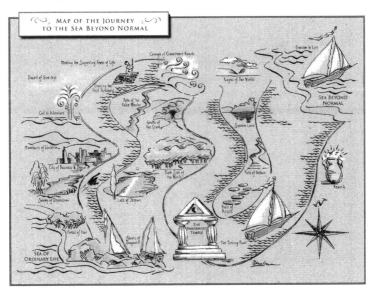

Figure 15. Map to the Sea beyond Normal

The Departure in this journey begins while we are still living our ordinary life. Before her diagnosis, Beth lived in what we might call stage 1, *The Ordinary World*. Beth defined herself as active, relatively secure, productive, and happy for the most part. She was rarely sick, ate well, exercised regularly, didn't smoke, had friends and family, and looked forward to the future. She was living under the spell of working for what we call "the good life."

I had lived in this state of "seeking the good life" before I woke up to the reality of what my first marriage really was. I lived in this state before I awakened to what being in the wrong career was doing to me. I needed these illusions to support my life and identity until I faced the deep, repressed emotions and scars from my childhood and adolescence. There are many examples of how such illusions as these are playing out in our lives and in the lives of the people around us.

This is the ordinary world before the beginning of the journey, when our identity, our place in life, our personal values and goals, our ideas of who "I" am, what "I" think "I" am, my vision of the future, my hopes, dreams, and longings all seem to be in place. The Departure from our ordinary world usually begins with an event—in Beth's case, a diagnosis—which we experience as a disaster. This is understood, in the deepest levels of our soul, to be a "call to adventure," according to Joseph Campbell.

This next stage—stage 2, *The Call to Adventure*—began when Beth's diagnosis stopped her cold from living in her ordinary world. Even though it took her some time to realize it, the psychological and emotional structures that provided meaning in her life disintegrated overnight. In these world-stopping experiences, we suddenly face a problem, a challenge, or the realization our life isn't what we thought it was. Sooner or later we will then realize that we are going to have to take risks if we want to further our lives. Beth's challenge here is clearly both her illness and the loss of the structures supporting her life and identity.

Decades ago, I faced the challenge of realizing that what could have been called a depression was my awareness that my life felt like it was drying up, dying like the wasteland in the King Arthur stories. In addition, these triggering events, situations, or losses are frequently seen as enemies or misfortunes rather than calls to adventure or teachers. And these events often touch on deeper fears, vulnerabilities, and even shame. Beth feared not being active and not being able to be an effective mother and a loving partner, and she felt ashamed of becoming needy. And I had a deep fear of cancer all my life that was rooted in the loss, terror, and abandonment felt by the child within me that I know so well. But these are all personal echoes of a universal pain that everyone can have or can suffer from. The question is whether we will begin the journey or retreat into a defensive shell.

◆ ◆ ◆

Well, the truth is that most of us initially enter stage 3, *Refusing or Accepting the Call to Adventure*, by refusing the call. After all, when we are really sick, we want to get well, or we want to lose weight, or we want to be happy, period. And yet deeper within us is this longing in our spirit for the vision of a journey toward greater meaning and a new life. There is a drive to come to a self we can only sense and to find renewed hope there.

Beth originally refused the call to a new life because she refused to accept the reality of her illness. And remember, as I said previously, that accepting doesn't mean giving into it or embracing it. Beth believed, as we are all taught to believe, that she could defeat it, overcome it, transcend it, or live on the shoulders of a positive attitude. Our reluctance to accept our situation and the call to adventure stems from our being called to face the unknown, the uncertainty of our lives, and our intense lack of true self-knowledge. In fact, as long as the emissary, the proponent of objectivity and rationality, rules our minds, we may not even trust the value of knowing ourselves.

In both our outer worlds and in the depth of our souls, we stand on the threshold of our greatest fears. At this point, the guardians that keep us from crossing the threshold into the journey toward adventure, toward a new life and radical hope, are *conventional wisdom* and *practical, conventional values*. These are the family, social, and religious ideals that make up our perceptions of what a good, rational person looks like who is in control and living a successful, conventional life. ***These guardians block us before we begin.*** And Beth, like many of us, had to find that only the depth of our despair finally gives us the strength to go through these blocks and other people's judgments. I have found in my decades of clinical experience that a persistent refusal of the call to adventure leads to a bitter and tragic fate. There is a sense of life being lost.

Thoughts and Questions to Ponder…

I shared that "the truth is that most of us initially enter stage 3, Refusing or Accepting the Call to Adventure, by refusing the call.

After all, when we are really sick, we want to get well, or we want to lose weight, or we want to be happy, period.

And yet deeper within us is also this longing in our spirit for the vision of a journey toward greater meaning and a new life.

There is a drive to come to a self we can only sense and to find renewed hope there."

What are your reflections about that?

The boundaries imposed from outside my self are the unexamined conventional wisdom and values and external ideals about what a good person is and what a good life is.

Am I feeling that those kinds of boundaries have been imposed upon me during my life?

Here are specific boundaries I have identified that do not feel helpful to my well-being and growth.

Here are some boundaries that keep me being my same old self with my same old unexamined attitudes and my same old unaddressed fears.

When I am ready, do I feel that I have developed the fortitude to pass through these old boundaries?

Observe and acknowledge how much these external boundaries shape your experiences and your life.

What do I feel when I meet the "guardians" of my boundaries?

Other thoughts…

CHAPTER 13

Commitment to the Journey Manifests Support

May courage
Cause our lives to flame,
In the name of the Fire,
And the Flame
And the Light.

— JOHN O'DONOHUE

I was very fortunate as I approached my surgery to have been asked to give the lecture I mentioned that was in the heart of my life's work. I had also been studying for almost a decade about the place of psychology in our experience of illness. There is no doubt that multiple factors go into the development of every illness. However, there is deep truth to what Dr. Jung says—that every illness has a strong psychological component. So it will greatly serve our life, our healing, and our individuation to explore this connection as thoroughly as we can. My more than thirty-five years of professional practice, which has included working with many people with illnesses, as well as my personal experiences, validate Dr. Jung's insight.

I also think that as we are struggling to accept the call, we also find out that Goethe, the great German poet, is right—the moment we commit ourselves fully, Providence moves too...we seem to find or simply run into helpful, supportive figures.

Accepting the call begins the Transformational phase of our journey with what I am calling stage 4, *Meeting the Supporting Power of Life.*

In Beth's case, stage 4, Meeting the Supporting Power of Life, was evidenced in her willingness to find and meet me and, by way of her encounter with me, to discover this path. It also included discovering the support from her dreams and her unconscious, especially her dream of the woman in the garden. Support comes from the outer world and from the depths within ourselves. At this stage, we are gaining the inner strength and confidence to begin the journey. And it is crucially important that our mentors be enthused about learning and living, for they must be a source of strength, wisdom, and support for us. False mentors can bog us down in traditional thinking and sentimentality, and they may be overly sympathetic to the initially overwhelming appearance of our situation.

Figure 16. Hidden Hands

As a matter of fact, I have to admit that books have often been my "mentors," as have lecture opportunities like the one I had in Washington, DC. I hope that this book can actually serve as a mentor and support for you. Our mentors seem to show up once we have accepted the call. Help seems to come from destiny, whether you call it the unconscious, the Self, the Divine, synchronicity, or all of the above. My experience of preparing and presenting my lecture in Washington, DC, confirmed for me Goethe's statement that the moment we commit ourselves fully, Providence moves too. Commitment brings us across the threshold as our journey opens, which I call stage 5, *Crossing the First Threshold*. Now the adventure feels dangerous because we have moved out of the familiar sphere of our old selves and community. We are crossing the boundary into our unconscious world as patients did when they entered the temple of Asclepius.

In dreams and myths, this crossing of the threshold is symbolized by such activities as plunging into the ocean, passing into the desert, getting lost in a dark forest, or finding ourselves in a strange city or a foreign land. The path may be an ascent toward heaven, but it more likely will be a descent, a journey into our darkest depths. Either way, it always goes beyond our current horizon. As Joseph Campbell notes, "It's always a path into the unknown, through the gateway, or the cave, or the clashing rocks." The clashing rocks in our case are the opposites of health and illness, and beyond them is the mystery of a greater life.

To take this actual first step requires acts of strength and bravery that support our commitment to healing and to seeking a new life. I have also taken this step when I felt like I had run out of other good options. In other words, desperation and terror have also turned out to be great motivators for me. They did the same for Beth as well when she acknowledged that she could not "defeat" her illness. Her realization of her reality helped her face the question, "Do I go on living my life as I am, or will I take the risks that are needed in order to make the effort to grow and change…to bring healing and love into my life and to transform my life?"

There are more threshold guardians confronting our progress, as Beth discovered when she had to face a father who was angry with her for getting sick, a mother who wanted to keep her fragile, and a medical system that all too often seemed to want to diminish her humanity.

Crossing this threshold prepares us for dying to our old selves in order for our new selves to be born. For this process to take place, we have to fully know the dimensions of our old selves in order to be sure they are not returning in the guise of something new. We have to get to know our old selves better by intentionally examining the assumptions and influences that have shaped who we are and how we live.

Figure 17. Angel Guarding Eden

Figure 18. Temple Guardians

Credit: Wikimedia Commons

Thoughts and Questions to Ponder...

As we look more deeply at the power of commitment and more actively take the steps that support our commitment to healing and to a new life, we acknowledge that this requires acts of strength and bravery.

Let's look again at some of the questions from chapter 4.

At this point in the journey, redefine for yourself what commitment means to you.

Committing to your self...to your own authentic self...is the beginning of the most important story of your life.

Can you begin to see this commitment to your authentic self as a love story?

Can you regard loving yourself as a sacred commitment?

Can you see that this ongoing love story of truly valuing yourself opens the way for you to love all that is...to love your big Self?

What does making an ongoing commitment to your own journey of healing feel like and look like? Identify some specific ways you can do this each day.

Have you been able to support yourself in these efforts to state the following sentences?

What are your feelings now about each statement?

I commit to being fully human.

*I accept that I am experiencing this illness,
and I commit to being open to my own transformation.*

*I choose to be a seeker of new and deeper
self-knowledge and consciousness.*

*I am continuing on my journey...and bring my resolve, my
willingness to stay the course to be my true, authentic self...*

*I commit myself to be and do what is best for me...to nurture
love, patience, persistence, acceptance, and respect for myself.*

Other thoughts...

CHAPTER 14

Full Engagement: Freeing the Master

When you travel
A new silence
Goes with you.
And if you listen,
You will hear
What your heart would
Love to say.

— JOHN O'DONOHUE

Credit: AngMoKio / Wikimedia Commons

Figure 19. Fu Dogs

In chapter 12, I mentioned the "gate guardians" that try to keep us from passing through the thresholds that lead to our healing and wholeness. I listed conventional wisdom, practical and conventional values, and family, social, and religious ideals that make up our perceptions of a good, rational person who is in control and living successfully by our societal standards.

We can expand these guardians into four basic fears that tend to keep us locked into our old selves:

The first fear is a basic fear of our emotions. We fear that they may overwhelm us, shame us, possess us, and make us look out of control and ridiculous. The reality is that as our society worships rationality and objectivity, we remain dull and maimed in our emotional capacities, like children who never developed. Even if we are considered very emotional, few of us have learned how to cultivate and mature our "feeling selves." From the Asklepion point of view or from the Master's perspective, understanding is not enough. Feeling is the point. Only emotions truly engage us in our experience of living. Understanding and experiencing are not interchangeable. We need them both. It is only through our cultivated emotions that we can carefully weigh our values in a way that can support and direct our lives.

The second fear that can block us is the fear that we will destroy the life we have carefully constructed and the values that we have embraced to support our lives. I understand this fear and have seen it many times. I once heard a woman say at a seminar, "I would rather die of cancer than get a divorce." A chill ran down my spine when I heard this comment, for it was not about love. In addition, in the face of a serious crisis or illness in a person's life, I have often seen that what was formerly very important to the person suddenly seemed strangely empty of value. The answer to responding to this second fear effectively lies in educating and maturing our feelings in order to free the Master from imprisonment.

The third fear that blocks many of us is that we will blame ourselves for our crisis or illness. People in our society blame themselves day in and day out because they feel like they are not getting life "right." Without educated emotions and feeling values, which include compassion, generosity, and gratitude, rationality turns on us, and from a position of "rationality," oversimplified "cause and effect" thinking compels us to blame ourselves. Beth once remarked to me, "I always knew I should have done better." Better than what? It probably doesn't matter "about what," since we tend to think that way about anything that goes wrong. Educated feelings help us be resilient and tough with ourselves. Rationality and objectivity by themselves rob us of our humanity and leave us no option but to be hard on ourselves. If you do that long enough and hard enough, you will get sick.

The fourth fear we have is one of embarrassment when we learn our emotions are in a primitive state. This state is a common one in this age when we worship thinking and learning and want experts to give us the answer to everything. This fear is humbling as well, because we can't educate our feelings in the ways we have been taught to learn other things. We must allow ourselves to "feel our feelings," and our felt experience of these emotions helps to cultivate and educate them. It is also important that we don't fall prey to the rational emissary and say to ourselves, "What good can these efforts do?" or "Is it worth all of this trouble?" These efforts are very important to our processes of healing and growth. In fact, they are key to this journey.

Yet we still have to be humble enough to begin this process like a child. As long as the emissary rules in our minds, we are in danger of having a major crisis or illness push us to the brink of hopelessness. A major shock can cause us the kind of fear and depression we never knew was possible. My first wife's initial schizophrenic episode was such a shock for me. I had no idea that this kind of thing was possible. The way I wanted people to see us outwardly disappeared in a heartbeat. In these times, most of us become depressed and worry about "losing everything" and life becoming "worthless." The emissary teaches us to hide our shock, pain, and grief. By doing this, it teaches us to have contempt for our psychic processes and our feelings, and our society shows little mercy on those of us who fail to do this. We learn to have self-loathing for our so-called feelings of weakness.

In one of our sessions, Beth told me, "I learned before I can even remember to never tell anyone what I really felt. I must have learned this almost as soon as I learned to talk. This was a lesson that left me constantly worried about what people would think and how much I could be hurt by them. It didn't take me too many years until I had learned to not even tell myself what I really felt."

Repressing our stronger emotions, like fear, anger, sadness, and despair, causes us to also lose touch with our capacities for inspiration, hope, and joy, which are some of our strongest healing potentials. The repression and denial of our genuine emotions also increase our alienation from our authentic personality potentials. Then our reality is that the more we are alienated from ourselves, the more subject we become to illness, and the more difficulty we have in getting well when we are sick. In Jungian terms, we include the home for these repressed emotions in our unconscious as part of our shadow.

When our early lives are rough and challenging and at times abusive, unloving, and isolating, as Beth's was, we are going to repress most of our emotions in order to feel safe and to not feel any more overwhelmed than we already are. Then, as adults, whenever stressful events come up in our lives, these old reactive patterns take over in our psyche. In addition, we will have developed a psychological pattern of living that is designed to protect us from the effects of events like those in our early lives, even though they are no longer a threat. A repressive, defensive style of living then becomes structured into our personality, as it had in Beth's.

The primary reason for this structure still being present is that the old emotions that we repressed as children are still alive in our psyche and patterned in our brains. When a child grows up under difficult circumstances, that child will build up a large reservoir of anger or fear or both. It's important to remember that there is no "timeline" in our unconscious. That reservoir of anger and fear will sit deep inside of us like a volcano until some event triggers an explosion of it.

Keeping these emotions repressed robs us of our vitality. Repression and denial take a lot of emotional energy. The cost to us is living with a constant amount of anxiety, fatigue, and depression that may have gone on so long that we are no longer aware of it. In addition, we are emotionally encapsulated and are unable to fully participate in loving relationships to the extent we really want and need to. Eventually, the repressed energy in these emotions may become manifested in addictions, psychological and physical symptoms, and illnesses. Simply becoming aware of these emotions and expressing them is not the answer. If we avoid reexperiencing how we felt and how these patterns continue, and we merely talk about them from a safe distance, nothing changes in either our psyche or neural pathways, and we have created a new defensive structure.

The true healing of problems is to go beneath the surface of our conscious minds and enter into the unconscious and explore our emotional wounds and experiences from within our emotional selves. By entering into the depth of our shadows, we are going into our emotions, the patterns they take on, and the expressions that lie beneath our conditioning and beyond our conscious awareness. The emotions lead us to the heart of the problem and the patterns of behavior that they now evoke. These patterns are also reflected in our neural pathways.

In his poem "Healing," D. H. Lawrence writes, "I am ill because of wounds to the soul, to the deep emotional self, and the wounds to the soul take a long, long, long time, only time can help and patience, and a certain difficult repentance, long difficult repentance, realization, of life's mistake, and the freeing oneself from the endless repetition of the mistake which mankind at large had chosen to sanctify." The origin of the word "repentance" is "to return." So we must return to the experiences of the emotions whose repression directed us away from our authentic selves. Becoming aware of them and accepting our experiences that generated them is moving into the "long difficult repentance" of restoring ourselves to ourselves.

Transforming these patterns transforms our lives. This work of transformation is hard, necessary, and rewarding. But we have to work at it in the same committed way that we would train for a marathon. We build up the emotional fitness for this work gradually through hard, personal work and emotionally lived experiences. Here are some of the methods we use and questions we ask ourselves to help us stop repeating the same mistaken patterns and to restore and cultivate our emotional selves. I will come back to these methods in more detail in chapter 23.

Journaling: A great deal of research now shows that keeping a daily journal about ourselves—our thoughts, feelings, and concerns—promotes good physical and emotional health. Journaling reflects our daily lives back to us and allows us to glimpse parts of ourselves we've hidden, to review our emotional response to daily events, and to open a field of perspective where our unconscious can emerge and our relationship to ourselves can become stronger. Our journal can also become the home for recording our dreams, fantasies, stories, and the other exercises I will suggest.

Acceptance: We must be open to accepting the emotions, thoughts, and memories that come up. We must also write them in our journal. This puts them into a concrete form, helps clarify them, and helps us relate to them more objectively. We give them expression by writing them down. They may also be expressed in other forms, such as art, sculpture, dance, and so on. These forms of expression may bring a sense of emotional release. They are not, though, transformative of the psychological patterns in our psyche and brain—these expressions must be carefully discussed with your analyst for real changes to take place.

Stories: We must tell the stories of our original wounding, of our driven journey, and of our misguided attempts to find healing. And we must avoid telling them from an intellectual viewpoint, like a "patient's history." We must tell the stories from inside our emotional self.

Important:

Don't try to do all of this at once. It takes time, like training for a marathon, to develop strength and endurance. The more we journal—the more we explore, develop, and amplify—the more psychologically fit we become for the marathon that is our life. But it is important that we sit down and think about these things every day and give them a concrete form as well by writing them in our journal. This is the way that ideas and feelings get from our shadow into our consciousness. This is how we change how we are living and restructure the patterns in our psyche and in the feelings in our bodies. Set aside time for these activities each day.

Challenging the gate guardians is actually challenging the limits of our current personality. They appear dangerous and arouse fear from our unconscious within us. Pushing these limits that grew to protect our vulnerability seems frightening and risky. But as we do so, our confidence will grow along with our courage, and the threat from these hidden parts of our history and development will fade.

Thoughts and Questions to Ponder...

Answer these "Helpful Questions for Reflecting and Journaling":

What kinds of things cause you stress?

What makes you angry or enraged?

What scares you and makes you feel vulnerable and insecure?

What do you worry the most about?

Who are the people who didn't treat you as well as you would have liked during your entire life? Start at the beginning.

What kind of stress affects you the most?

What kind of pain do you experience, and what connections does it have to your emotions?

As you reflect on these questions and write about them, try to amplify your thoughts and answers by including the context, history, the details, and the story of what is coming up in your answers.

Reflecting and Journaling on Your Personality:

Am I a perfectionist?

Do I expect a great deal from myself?

Am I my own biggest critic?

Am I oversensitive to criticism?

Do I have a strong need to please people?

Who is it hard for me to confront and when?

Is it difficult for me to figure out what I need—and ask for it?

Am I a "caretaker"?

Do I want people to like me, and do I tend to be overly helpful?

Am I overcontrolling?

Again, these are questions to write about and expand on.

Include your thoughts about the place of these questions in your own history, about the details and stories around them.

All of these personality traits have the potential to cause us to amass repressed anger in our shadows. Needing to be too good, too controlled, and having trouble with confrontations are common and build up emotions in our shadows.

Feelings of inferiority that may be revealed by some of these questions also cause us to accumulate reservoirs of rage, despair, and shame.

Reflecting and Journaling on Life Pressures:

Do you feel pressure in your job?

Do you feel pressure from your partner?

Do you feel pressure from your family?

Do you feel pressure from your parents?

Do you feel pressure from finances?

Do you feel pressure from any other big aspects of your life?

Do you feel pressure from your age?

Make a list of the situations where you feel angry and cannot express it, whatever the reasons may be.

Once again, amplify and develop your thoughts around each of these questions, the details around the answers, and the stories connected to them.

Notice if the patterns are repeating.

How do you feel as you are writing about these pressures?

Other thoughts...

CHAPTER 15

The Road of Trials

You barely noticed how each day opened
A path through fields never questioned,
Yet expected, deep down, to hold treasure.
Now your time on earth becomes full of threat;
Before your eyes your future shrinks.

– JOHN O'DONOHUE

Now let us continue with the next stage on our mythic journey of initiation, our journey toward healing and wholeness and what the author Reynolds Price called "a whole new life" after his experience of cancer that left him paraplegic. Stage 6 is called *The Road of Trials.*

The Road of Trials takes us beyond the rational approach to healing and truly into the Asklepion approach or individuation, where we enter a new landscape where psyche and soma are inherently linked, where life is lived more symbolically, and where paradox seems to reign. The roles of the principles and values in our former identities seem reversed, and accepting these paradoxes involves tests that often seem impossible to us. Frequently we are confused and disoriented. And we find that we have often made enemies out of people who have either refused the call to self-awareness and transformation in their own lives or who have repressed it. They want us to be the person we always have been and to continue the old games and roles we played with them.

There is much more to this road of trials, and at this point, I want to share another one of Beth's dreams that shows how we may have to confront the unlived life, the unrealized potentials and repressed emotions within ourselves—our shadows. Beth had a dream in which her old house had collapsed as if being demolished by a tornado.

In the next scene in the dream, she was entering a new house. Its form was vague, but as she went in, she immediately opened a door and began a long descent into a dusky basement. She followed a dim source of light until she came into a room made of stone, with ancient wooden furniture. Sitting at a table was a woman who was darkly beautiful, even sexy, with flowing black hair down to her waist. She was dressed in a cascading, form-revealing material, and while she was beautiful and sexy, her nails were sharp as daggers, and her eyes glinted as if hiding fire. Beth said, "I knew I was in dangerous territory, and yet I felt a certain kind of fascination with her." Beth also said that she felt as though she was about to seek the heart of her inner world and perhaps the heart of her illness. She remembered my words that as we pursue this journey, we must be both brave and humble. We have to beware of illusions from our past and new threshold guardians from the conventional world. And as we do our work, we must face some things without help, and our resistances and fears may have to be overcome with a forceful act of strength. Beth found herself in that situation as she decided to dialog with this woman.

Figure 20. A Tornado

Credit: Justin Hobson, Justin1569 at English Wikipedia

As I share her dialog with you, I want to remind you that I will discuss this dialog technique more fully later. Beth told me that she was scared before she sat down and began writing this dialog.

The dialog opened with Beth saying:

Beth: Well, I guess you are my shadow. Who are you really? What's your name?

Woman: Are you sure you want to know? I have many shapes and names.

Beth: I am afraid. I'm not sure.

Woman: That shows you have some sense of whom you're dealing with. I think you realize I have the power to be creative or destructive and to love and hate passionately. Are you sure you want to know me?

Beth: Are you playing games with me?

Woman: No. I'm asking you a direct question.

Beth: Yes, but I'm still afraid of what I might find out.

Woman: So much fear. Fear can control us. Does your fear control you?

Beth: Oh, yes!

Woman: How does it make you feel?

Beth: Helpless, weak, sick, out of control.

Woman: Fear is one of my faces, and I live deep in your foundations.

Beth: Will you tell me where you came from?

Woman: Actually I am more than just fear. I'm the part of you that has carried every defeat and death in your life until now. Of course, I'm talking symbolically here. Every blow to your nature and character, however small and subtle, and however large, has accumulated in me over time. Imagine how many years we are talking about here.

Beth: *(crying)* Oh, God. It hurts to think about it.

Woman: Of course it hurts. Because I am fed up, I'm furious. Do you think I want to carry this load forever? I want to be set free.

Beth: Have I imprisoned you?

Woman: Not really. You just haven't fought hard enough to let me live.

Beth: But to live in what way? Who are you?

Woman: I'm not sure I want to tell you.

Beth: Don't play games. Be direct.

Woman: My name. Hmmm. Yes, I am you. My name is Beth.

Beth: You are me?

Woman: Yes, it's hard to understand, isn't it?

Beth: You are the real me?

Woman: Now you are catching on. I am the real you.

Beth: So then who am I?

Woman: You are not so dense after all…You are not yourself, that's for sure. But I am not really that interested in who you are. You are some strange mixture of who you think you are meant to be…who you were told to be. I think you get the picture.

Beth: Yes. So who are you really? Or perhaps I should ask, who am I really?

Woman: One step at a time. You need to work on these thoughts and then come back to see me again. Remember, we'll take this one step at a time, and then I can be helpful.

Beth: Thank you. Let me give this some time to sink in, and I'll get back to you.

As Beth and I talked more after this dialog, she told me: "You know, I have what I think of as an adaptive complex. It means that I grew up trying to get love and affirmation by trying to please everyone. Later on, trying to please turned into achieving in school and then taking charge of situations, solving problems, and making everything work for everybody. I have become very proud of my abilities to do this. I feel special in my own mind."

132

Beth continued, "But while I was proud, I was also vulnerable, and I was building up a reservoir of fear and anxiety. What if I failed? What if I make a mistake? What if I did something wrong? What if I end up feeling sad, lonely, and afraid? Can I keep up this pace? Will I end up all alone and unloved?...You see how this chain of fear keeps spiraling down. I also realize these are reasons I am afraid to confront people. I never learned, and nobody ever taught me how to take up for myself. I even think just making a direct statement of what I think or want is an aggressive act. No wonder my shadow is so furious."

◆ ◆ ◆

My understanding of the shadow aspect in our personalities has continued to evolve for over forty years. Daily in my life and work, I am impressed by the power in this aspect of our unconscious as it operates within us as a repository for unexpressed, unacknowledged feelings and desires. It contains a force that accumulated tremendous energy, and our efforts to keep this energy repressed rob us of just as much energy, perhaps even more energy. The emotional power in our shadow builds up when we fail to face our wounds, learn from our suffering, honor our gifts, follow the calls of our muses, and discover the potentials meant to be lived through us.

Our shadows have a great but often unseen power, operating on deep, interior levels, to communicate with us. They may be sabotaging our efforts, upsetting our balance, fueling our weight and addictions, sapping our energy, and even making us sick. In other words, we must live in a way that expresses our true nature and our potentials for love and vitality or begin to rigidify, wither, and die.

From this touching and dramatic dialog and our discussion, we see Beth's approach through a door opened by a dream. It takes her to her innermost self, to some of the truths about her life, and to her potentials for growth. Facing the truth of our own reality, the truth about our experiences, and the deep pain and anger within us—what Dr. Jung calls the confrontation with our shadow—is indeed scary and is a humiliating road of trials. Yet it is also exciting as we learn that realizing our potential healing of ourselves and strengthening our personality—in other words, becoming an authentic person—depend upon our willingness to begin to see the world through our own eyes.

Beth and I worked with this shadow figure for quite a while, and this figure returned as a teacher and a presence in Beth's future inner work and with her illness. This work led to the next phase in our inner journey that I call stage 7, *The Approach to the Innermost Temple.*

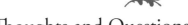

Thoughts and Questions to Ponder...

Joseph Campbell tells us that the hero or heroine's journey "is always a path into the unknown, through the gateway, or the cave or the clashing rocks." Passing through this gateway prepares us for dying to our old selves in order for our new selves to be born.

What are your feelings about this?

For this process to take place, we have to fully know the dimensions of our old selves in order to be sure they are not returning in the guise of something new.

Do you feel you are beginning to know the dimensions of your old self?

We get to know our old selves better by intentionally examining the assumptions and influences that have shaped who we are and how we live.

What are some assumptions and beliefs that have shaped your present mind-set?

Do you have a sense that you are ready to face your wounds?

Are there any insights that you have learned from your suffering?

Do you feel that you can honor your gifts and discover the potentials meant to be lived through you?

Are there values and principles you took for granted that you are now reevaluating?

Other thoughts...

CHAPTER 16

The Approach to the Innermost Temple

May you keep faith with your body,
Learning to see it as a holy sanctuary
Which can bring this night-wound gradually
Toward the healing and freedom of dawn.

— JOHN O'DONOHUE

Approaching the Temple is the symbolic passage into accepting that there is a force within me that is greater than I am, and it is wanting me to live in a way that not only desires for me to fulfill the unique potentials of my life; it wants me to fulfill potentials I haven't even known I have. Dr. Jung writes that our encounters with the Self are a defeat for our current identity and self-image. This defeat teaches us that no matter how empowered we think we are, how much in control we think we are, how much we think we can create our own lives, we are wrong. Nothing can teach us this fact faster or humble us more than the diagnosis of a major illness.

The purpose of this defeat is to redirect us and open us into...and put us in search of...the most profound values that we can live. This defeat can also open us to the truest parts of ourselves that are meant to be recognized and expressed through our lives. The purpose of the defeat is to reorient our attitudes toward ourselves and life. Dr. Frankl summed up this experience by saying that we must learn that it doesn't really matter what we expect from life. What matters, he says, is what life expects from us. Instead of passively wondering why these things happened to me, or what the meaning of my life or illness is, we need to learn that we are being questioned daily and hourly by life and by the big Self, the container of the life force within us.

This reality means we are being called to act...to become seekers. We must look for the answers to what is life expecting from us through our seeking the support and guidance of the Self. We need to listen to the inner voice of the Self coming to us through reflecting upon our experiences, our situations, our emotions, our illnesses, and our shadows. Every time we face one of these questions, one of these crushing questions on the surface of our lives, we must realize that it is unique.

My cancer was a unique question from life because it was and is my question. I must discover the more profound answers from the big Self and take responsibility for the seeking, for living the answers, and for fulfilling the challenges and tasks that life has set before me. There are no shortcuts. The journey begins and opens through knowing our shadow. You see in Beth's dream, and through our dialogs with our pain and illnesses, that this is true. These, too, are parts of our shadow. It may seem like a paradox that our wholeness may come from our most humiliating and frightening experiences, as I found with my cancer. But the real truth is in what the experience of cancer generated and renewed in me.

To begin with, in an illness as serious as cancer, we are slammed with great emotions that we need to learn to assimilate and transform. To accomplish this, we may have to go far back into the history of our lives. As we do this, it is important to remember that only our emotions can fully engage us in life to the point that we can even hear the questions that life is asking us. Then, through our relationship with the Self, we begin to realize that as we try to create our lives as an expression of the Self, we are being created. As we try to express the big Self, we become expressed in ways we could never have imagined. As we seek to discover meaning, we become more meaningful. Soon we realize that our journey is what matters, what grounds us in our place in the mystery of life.

Approaching the Temple is an act of turning myself over to life and to the big Self and of helping my experiences and the big Self form me. The Self is the part of me, perhaps, that is beyond all names and all doctrines. For me, it is the only experience that I truly, personally have of what I call God or the Divine. Approaching the Temple is approaching the ground for that experience. In the Temple, I am standing on holy ground. Just as Moses was instructed to do, I must take off my shoes and stand barefoot, humbled, and in awe because I will learn again that there is a bigger power directing my life.

I learned this reality while facing my first wife's schizophrenia. I learned it again in my thirties, when I had not only achieved "success" but found it empty, and an inner voice was telling me I would have a heart attack before I was forty if I didn't radically change my life. I had it again when my daughter was diagnosed with MS, and again when I was diagnosed with cancer. Actually, these are the major events marking a renewed quest each time. I have had a number of smaller versions of the same pattern. Every time, I stood in the Temple barefoot on holy ground. I also faced a burning bush whose voice was demanding that I answer the questions life was asking me, that cracked my self-image and humbled me. I was humbled because I was being asked to do things I didn't know if or believe that I could do. I had never planned or consented to this path that I knew of, and the only decision I could make was to accept it or not. But I slowly and painfully discovered that embarking on this journey transformed me and enlarged me, even as it humbled me and disrupted my self-image.

The journeys have done more than that. They have led me into a life that is far beyond what I could have planned or imagined, where love, happiness, and joy are enfolded in my daily living, along with suffering, pain, and sorrow. Now let me take us back to the point where we are approaching the Temple.

Figure 21. The Temple

139

At this point in the journey, we are still in scary emotional territory. We are about to seek the heart of our inner world and what triggered our inner journey. Beth, and I as well, were seeking the heart of our illness. We had to be both brave and humble. And I was certainly scared. We had to beware of illusions from our past and new threshold guardians from the conventional world. And like us, as you do your work, you must face some things without help, and your resistance and fear may have to be overcome with a forceful act of strength. This happened to me when I made my first dialog with my cancer after summoning the courage and willpower to take this step.

As I share this dialog with you, I want to mention that I originally tried to dialog with my prostate before my diagnosis, but the image of the word cancer kept coming up instead, in spite of my history with that word and how much I hated and feared it.

Bud: What drives the engine of your presence?

Cancer: All the love you needed and didn't get, all the understanding you needed and didn't get, all the safety you needed and didn't get.

Bud: Haven't I worked on myself for decades to love, heal, and awaken myself and all of that?

Cancer: Yes, you have. That's why you are facing me now—the image that killed your mother—that made up your father's last battle when he was neutered by retirement. Why do you think I visit men in the organ that releases their creativity?

Bud: Is this a final challenge?

Cancer: There are no final challenges. It is a challenge at the heart of your creativity. One that is generational, cultural, and personal. Your challenge is to more consciously serve the Self, life. To do this, you have to root out this image of me—its grandiose growth and grandiose outer stuff, like remodeling the house, moving, or taking a fantasy spiritual pilgrimage.

Bud: Yes, I know, but you sneak up on me. You are like a troll under a bridge. I was even thinking of making this dialog into a book.

Cancer: Do I jump out at you, or is that your defense?

Bud: Defense against what?

Cancer: Against facing the hard inner work, dying, and changing.

Bud: I think I've done a lot of that.

Cancer: Not enough!

Bud: I will have to be held down—worked on by a robot—sidelined for weeks.

Cancer: Maybe it's safer to sideline yourself—write every night, get to know me. Think about your dad. Why was he stuck in his job, afraid? Why couldn't he confront his second wife and his mother and insist that his children be loved? Why did he want to fight so much of his life?

Bud: Why couldn't I?

Cancer: You were too unconscious and had no model.

Bud: I wanted to be reborn into the world without using you. I know you helped me at times. But you also hurt me, robbed me of real life.

Cancer: True, but real life is practical—difficult, and it includes many deaths.

Bud: So does being too strong. Let's stop for now. I'm exhausted.

I think you can see from my dialog that we are almost in shamanic territory here. I am on a symbolic line between life and death. I'm approaching the central crisis in this transformation in my illness. After this initial dialog, I was exhausted. Then I realized that I had actually had a dialog with my cancer. I had learned new things from it, and it wasn't as demonic as I pictured it. I've had more dialogs and more help from it. I often think of myself as an artist in the art of living. Artists are not intentionally creative. They are receptive to the creativity that wants to flow through them into expression. The same is true for me, and the energy comes from the big Self.

Like any artist, I must be constantly creating and re-creating—that is, I must be constantly creating and re-creating myself. My cancer was telling me I was in a rut. I had stopped the process of creating and re-creating. In other words, I was simply living a life of repeating myself—and repeating oneself, for an artist, is dying. This is where my Temple is, and it is scary, exciting, and challenging. It is important for you to find your Temple as well. This book is meant to be a road map for doing that. The people in this book are examples of our possibilities, and yet, as you see, the journey is always a unique and very personal one.

Thoughts and Questions to Ponder...

At the very core of my own being, this is where my Temple is… and it is scary, exciting, and challenging.

What does being at the center of my own center feel like?

Approaching the Temple is an act of turning myself over to life and to the big Self, and helping my experiences and the big Self form me.

How am I feeling about that? What are my resistances?

The big Self is the part of me that is beyond all names and all doctrines.

Do I have a sense of that? Can I develop a deeper understanding of that?

In the Temple, I am standing on holy ground.

What does sacred, holy ground mean to me?

In the Temple, you can begin to see your illness in a new light and dialog with it.

Other thoughts...

CHAPTER 17

The Turning Point:
Listening to the Burning Bush

The hunger of Fire has no need
For the reliquary of the future;
It adores the eros of now,
Where the memory of the earth
In flames that lick and drink the air
Is made to release

Its long-enduring forms
In a powder of ashes
Left for the wind to decipher.
                 – JOHN O'DONOHUE

O ur journey intensifies as we enter stage 8…what I'm going to call *The Turning Point*, or what Joseph Campbell calls the Supreme Ordeal. This is the point when we have entered the Temple and are standing on holy ground. While I am in the inner Temple, I begin my approach to facing myself by asking, "Why am I ill?" The question really is, "Why am I ill, beyond the biology of the situation?"

If I am going to look at myself and my illness wholistically, in terms of body, mind, and spirit, it is important for me to consider a number of things. Of course, I must consider toxic environments, food, water, and air, and also consider viruses, genetic vulnerabilities, and dispositions and other biological questions. There are many factors that combine to cause an illness.

But in the Temple, I must ask the question, "Why am I ill?" to mind and spirit as well as body. The Jungian approach gives us the means to ask these questions. It is the wisdom we gain from asking these questions, and the journey of listening to the answers, that teaches us what to do with our knowledge and how to listen to and aid our inner nature in its healing efforts.

In many ways, this is when we touch the bottom. We come face to face with ourselves, our shadow, and experience our encounter with the Self, the eternal, the Divine. We finally comprehend that the archetypal pattern of transformation—life, death, and rebirth—is real and that we, our egos, experience the death portion as chaos, pain, conflict, betrayal, illness, and despair. We also recognize that we can't work through life conceptually. Slowly we begin to realize that the dark woods of our experiences that seemed so hostile to us, that made us terrified and unsure of ourselves, give way to a different kind of darkness, one that can be the womb for the birth of a renewed life. But for this to happen, we must first experience our life fully, ground our emotions in reality, and stand firm in them, neither being swallowed up by them nor denying them. The Jungian writer Florida Scott Maxwell said we must accept that "life does not accommodate you, it shatters you. It is meant to, and couldn't do it better. Every seed destroys its container or there would be no fruition." This is the secret of the ordeal—can we die to the old and be reborn?

It was while I was still in the Temple and still facing the burning bush that I had my second dialog with cancer. Its voice continued to be the voice from the burning bush that scorched and challenged me. The dialog went like this:

Bud: OK, Cancer, I've finally got up the nerve to come back. What I'm still facing scares the shit out of me. What is the hard work and changing I am afraid to face?

Cancer: You're right to be scared. You've had a hard recovery physically and emotionally. But you are one stubborn son of a bitch to change. You need to accept your ability to *shine*, to live and work slowly, like you did today; to be thorough—to treat all of your teaching and your students with deep respect. You tend to get your attitude all wrong.

Bud: Yes.

Cancer: You see this as hard work, depriving you of being what?

146

Lazy? It is not hard work. It is living with love, filling yourself, and then giving it away, loving your life, and then letting it find you.

Bud: I know I see this work as a burden—but it's slowly changing as I realize I can accomplish it without being driven and in fact without being afraid of being overwhelmed and unappreciated. And I still battle my inertia.

Cancer: You'd better win that battle, or your creativity will back up inside of you and become dark—fearful—sublimated into grandiose ideas—Ha!—cancer—I will be invited back. You have to change. My astrological symbol is the crab, and crabs have to shed their old shells and grow. So do you.

Bud: You have no mercy on me.

Cancer: That's not so. We said this journey into illness began with the love you needed and didn't get, the affirmation you needed and didn't get. This work is an expression of love, and you are getting love and affirmation. Let yourself feel it.

Feel the love from Massimilla and your children. Feel the affirmation in the lives you've helped change.

Bud: I do, more than ever.

Cancer: Yes, but open yourself to more…and to more friendship. Plus you are just beginning to touch the love from your unconscious, your Self, your soul, God.

Bud: I am still too proud. I am human. I know you are right, but I must say please don't hurt me anymore.

Cancer: I can't promise that. I can only help you find meaning, purpose, and love.

Bud: Damn, this is exhausting, difficult. Life is hard. God, please help me. Help me have courage to follow, to be receptive, even if I am sick.

These two dialogs were the first of many. But they were the ones that took place in the Temple. Speaking to cancer in these dialogs was like speaking to the burning bush, and they became a turning point. I remembered that when Moses faced the burning bush, the voice of the Divine coming from it gave him a significant task: "Set my people free."

In my own case, I interpreted my dialog to be telling me to set free the potentials in myself that I had been denying and to eliminate the oppressive fears and conditioning that were keeping me away from the "promised land," my deepening relationship with my greater Self.

The symbolic meanings of illness and transformation certainly scared me at first. That is one of the reasons why I tried so hard to understand them. It was after these two dialogs that I realized I was not being attacked by my cancer. I was being challenged to become more fully human, to be more assertively alive, and to enter into the death phase of the approach to a new life as the beginning of the death-and-re-creation pattern.

As you might imagine, I was surprised to learn that my cancer was telling me that I became sick because I was unable to go on with my needed development. New growth energy pushes toward being recognized and wants us to actualize it. If we can recognize it and live into it, a restructuring and rebirthing of our personality, our small self, takes place. This process doesn't stop with age and can catch any of us unaware. This place of my greatest vulnerability became a holy place, a place of healing and transformation. It became a place in which miracles could take place. From this turning point forward, healing became a renewed devotion of trying to listen to, experience, and incorporate every hint and every message that my big Self is sending to me.

I dedicate the final chapters in this book to further explaining how I discerned these messages. Listening to every hint and message from my inner big Self has become central to my approach to living and developing the potentials inherent in my life that my big Self is striving to fulfill. This is has become my way of life.

As challenging as this task is, I insist upon approaching it in a receptive manner that is open, relaxed, intensely curious, and sometimes scared. But I am seeking to be led, not to lead or to "take control" of my life. In other words, I have to remain humble and be sure my type A and left-brain tendencies that have meant a lot to me in the past are now serving a greater sense of value and purpose. As I listen and live this way, I am constantly reassured that something deep within me cares about me and my life.

The turning point was the beginning of a deep and ongoing conversation with my emotions, my unconscious, my body, and my big Self. It has become, as I have shared, a way of life that is not driven, overscheduled, or anxious. It is the centerpiece of how I live. Paradoxically, following this path has expanded my experiences of life as well as my accomplishments, many of which I could never have planned.

◆ ◆ ◆

Beth's Dialog

When Beth faced the burning bush, the first thing that swept over her was her fear. Here is what she said to her lesions…

Beth: I'm so afraid of you. You are making me lose control of my body. I'm even more afraid that my mind is slowing down. What if everything just stops?

Lesions: You are right to be scared. You've taken a long time to get around to listening to me. I want your full attention, your devotion. Perhaps then some other things can fall into place.

Beth: You mean healing will begin…

Lesions: Not so fast. You have a lot more to learn about us, and yourself.

Beth: I've also been scared to face you because I have some ideas what you're about.

Lesions: You think so. Let's hear it.

Beth: It's about me being a pleaser, wanting to take charge of everything, and even feel good about how competent I am, and how I can anticipate everyone else's needs and take care of them better than they can.

Lesions: Good points. But you've already taken charge again.

Keep it up and I'll slap you good. I'm in charge here, and you'd better listen to me.

Beth: I'm sorry. Please go on.

Lesions: You're one of the most hyperactive, driven women I've ever seen. You are so rigid and idealistic I can't stand you. I'll make you shit in your pants. You've wanted everything too quickly and to be too damn nice. You have overworked us—your immune system—for years. Don't you get it—we're exhausted. You have also squashed the fact that you have lived with a hidden sense of intense anxiety for decades. So there!

Beth: Shit! I'm overwhelmed. You are raging like a fire out of control. I have to stop. I want to talk to Bud. I will come back. I know I must.

Beth did talk to me, and she did come back to her dialogs. She quickly began to see how her old attitudes needed to be changed, and how she needed to create a healing environment around her and within herself. Facing the burning bush, the voice of anger in her illness, helped her feel a new sense of self-confidence and direction in her life. Her illness wasn't cured, but her healing was reaching a new level.

◆ ◆ ◆

Not everyone is able to have such dialogs. That's OK; we all not all meant to be the same. The important point is to find a way that we can come into a deep conversation with ourselves. Nancy, a high school teacher with ulcerative colitis, began this process by dancing. At first, she just danced. The more she danced, the more emotions began to well up. Then, as she danced her emotions, she became closer and closer to her pain. Soon she was dancing with her disease. Then she found herself dancing *as* her disease, expressing it. She realized at this point that she was dancing in her Temple, and she began to journal her emotions and the experiences she was having.

Robert, a middle-aged physician who was having panic attacks, arrived in his Temple through working with a dream image. In one of his dreams, he knew there was a terrible, angry beast, something like a Tasmanian devil, living in the woods behind his house. He began writing in his journal about how much he feared this beast, its rage, and its out-of-control, destructive potentials. As he wrote about the beast and its raging potentials, he began to think about how much rage and aggression he had fought to control and repress all of his life. These thoughts reminded him of how aggressive he was as a small child, biting, screaming, and refusing to be potty trained. While writing, he began to cry as he realized how desperate this little boy had been—and still was, in his unconscious. As time went by, the more he wrote, the less frequent his attacks became. Soon it almost seemed natural for him to ask the beast, "Why are you here?" and "What can I do for you?"

Angela was a nurse who had always loved to read. She had suffered from a severe skin rash that had come and gone without an obvious cause since she was an early adolescent. Angela particularly liked to read plays, and she was in a local theater group. She decided to write a play with her rash as a major character. Then she had to imagine what her rash would say if it had its own voice. She also had to imagine how it would react and express itself in dialogs with others during a stream of situations. Soon Angela found herself in her Temple, amazed at what her rash was saying.

The important point in this approach to knowing ourselves and our illness is to create a field in our imagination where we can meet and listen to our illness and to what our big Self can say to us through it.

◆ ◆ ◆

After another dialog, Beth wrote in her journal, "Entering the darkness is not to simply reenact my past or my trauma and pain. It is a quest to know and acknowledge the truth of my own life, to discover and learn to love my destiny, and to do this by the way of making this a quest for the will of the spirit that gives meaning to my life."

After reading this to me Beth said, "This damned never-ending struggle to accept the transforming meaning of my illness led me into a confrontation with the beautiful and the horrible in my ordinary world. It isn't the greed and evil in the world that has torn me up—it is the suffering and the loveliness in my life and in the lives of those I know and love. The fear of seeing this suffering and loveliness kept my eyes closed in denial for a long time. Seeing the beautiful and the horrible, the suffering and the loveliness—in my life; not in Africa, not in Somalia, but in my life—flies in the face of our everyday desires and notions of the good life."

Thoughts and Questions to Ponder…

I feel like I've shared a lot with you. Sit back and relax a minute, take a couple of deep breaths, and then share some of your responses.

How do you understand the approach to the inner temple?

What thoughts or feelings came up in you around the turning point?

Were you surprised at anything I shared with you?

What are you feeling about Florida Scott Maxwell's statement, "Every seed destroys its container or there would be no fruition"?

This is the secret of the ordeal—can we die to the old and be reborn?

What are your feelings about this?

To accept the meaning of one's illness as being transformative often leads to an inner confrontation…Are you feeling a sense of that within you?

Other thoughts…

CHAPTER 18

The Return: New Life and Perspective

The heavy dark falls back to earth
And the freed air goes wild with light,
The heart fills with fresh, bright breath
And thoughts stir to give birth to color.

— JOHN O'DONOHUE

In the Temple we face the full awareness that life has given us a staggering blow that ends our former life and initially fails to offer us anything in the way of a new life that we can think of wanting. Yet if we are aware of the Jungian approach, we learn that this isn't the whole story. Inch by inch, we discover the hidden hands within our spirit, our big Self that can support us.

Figure 22. Hidden Hands

155

Inch by inch in most cases, yet in an instant flash in others...we hear the call to choose life by beginning to say, "The old Bud is dead. Who will I be now? How can I get there?" Surprisingly, we find that even our illness can give us some directions and a clear-eyed view of our reality, a view we have been busy denying and repressing for a long time. Illness is forcing us to change our lives. But once I and the other people I've worked with accepted that this change is inevitable, and that we must listen to what our bodies, our illnesses, and our big Self are trying to tell us, then a path appeared. Grief for the passing of an old self, of our old life and personality, is necessary. But grief is tricky. It must be experienced fully, but we must not get caught or bogged down in it. We must give it its due and then choose life.

On the road back, I changed not only how I listened to and devoted myself to my inner life, I made dramatic outer changes as well. I resigned from several professional organizations. I gave up my participation in analyst-training programs, and I quit traveling to lecture. I needed the new time to express what my big Self was urging me to live. I also needed to open my life, which meant to get the pressure out of it in order to be receptive to the creative expressions that wanted to form and evolve through me. The same thing happened with Dr. Jung after his heart attack in his sixties. He retired from his professional practice, devoted himself to expressing his inner Self, and wrote his best books after he was seventy.

While we are in the Temple, we realize that no matter how much we want to be the person we used to be, it is not going to happen. But if we are devoted to this path, we also discover that we are not alone. We have the history of the human experience itself that we are becoming part of...and we have the hidden hands that can support us...that can rise from our big Self, if we seek them and are open to them.

In my book *The Fire and the Rose: The Wedding of Spirituality and Sexuality*, I share that four truths have become apparent to me in my own pursuit of self-knowledge as a way of life:

First, I have learned that the fundamental assertion in most mystical traditions—that self-knowledge is the way to come to know the Divine—is absolutely true. Self-knowledge releases us from the prison of our personal history, deconditions us from the attitudes of our parents and society, and forces us to work through our losses, hurts, and grief. This act of purification, as the mystics called it, opens us to our depths, to the Self, the Divine energy within us.

The second truth I realized is that compassion must begin with myself. The cultivation of compassion toward my failures, shortcomings, and humanness opens the door to self-love and makes me a truly compassionate person with others. This process grounds us in our full humanity and supports the self-love implied in the commandment, "Love your neighbor as yourself." Self-love anchored in self-knowledge is the underpinning of how well we can give and receive love. Without self-love, our structure of relationships will crumble under the pressure of the smallest storms, and our so-called unselfish acts will create an inner cauldron of resentment. I know this from the results of many years when I thought I could be hard on myself and loving to others. The only person I fooled was myself. Self-love is like water flowing into a pond. When the pond is full, the water will overflow and begin to venture into the world. If we fail to know and love ourselves, we risk causing our souls to become arid and our hearts to stagnate in fear and defensiveness. What a wonderful paradox—loving ourselves is actually taking care of others.

The third thing I discovered is that a life based on the pursuit of self-knowledge continually takes us back into the world and among our communities. We cannot live a wholehearted life alone. We must participate in all the various relationships—attractions, love, friendships, conflicts, projections—to gain stimulation as well as the content that informs much of our search for self-knowledge.

The fourth and final thing that I gradually became aware of is that something inside me cares about me and my life. If I listen, it speaks to me through my dreams, fantasies, inspiration, and thoughts. When I reflect, journal, and work with my active imagination, it helps heal my wounds, turns my symptoms and failures into lessons, and aids me in discerning what my soul wants for my life. It does not save me from any of life's difficulties or catastrophes. But when I am suffering, it is there with me.

◆ ◆ ◆

Throughout the course of this book, I have called this something inside of me that cares about me and my life the Self. As an analyst, I have studied and worked with the concept of the Self for many years. I've seen its validity by noting how it works in my life and in the lives of the people I counsel professionally. Today, I experience the Self very personally instead of viewing it from the distance of psychological theory. While I am not a theologian, I believe that my interactions with the Self are a true experience of feeling the love of the Divine.

While struggling along in midlife, I realized that the better I knew myself, the more my actions were my own and not those of the actor I had been trained to be. This helped me understand that, like our shadows, our ego—our small self—is something we *have* and is simply part of our psyche. It isn't *who we are*, although it may feel that way. As part of our psyche, our small self has two purposes. The first is to give us an identity structure that enables us to live satisfactorily in the world. The second is to become the vehicle with which we discover our unfolding inner world by bringing it into the light of consciousness.

As our development progresses, we become more alive day by day, and our personality continues to become or expand. We become increasingly aware of who we really are and of the big Self seeking incarnation through us. As the ego and Self come into relationship, the result is a unified personality, which makes living not only an art but also a sacred act.

In a culture dominated by the emissary, our rational "cause and effect" approach to life, suffering, and bothering other people has become degrading and embarrassing. Even our prosperity religions and our new age magical thinking contribute to making our experiences of suffering something to be ashamed of. As the emissary's attitudes shape our lives, we see life as functional and lose our sense of the precious quality of a life well lived. The emissary's approach to life also literalizes how we see ourselves, as well as how we see our sacred books and traditions. This approach robs us of the rich symbolism in our dreams, traditions, and rituals. It also robs us of the sublime symbolism in our mythic and religious traditions and in our sacred books. The perspective of the Master and our greater Self helps us see through and beyond our ordinary experiences of life into the deeper meanings in these areas that are inexpressible in rational language and yet can bring meaning, support, and purpose to us.

The reality of this journey is that suffering can touch the depths of the human spirit, and "bothering" others gives them the choice to put aside their societal indoctrination, become inspired, and uncover their depths of compassion. Suffering can ennoble all of us instead of degrading the sufferer. In truth, I have seen accepting suffering bravely and seeking a new vision of life and meaning affect people profoundly a number of times.

The Return begins with forming a new perspective, developing a new vision of the future, as Tom Swift did when he wrote in our local newspaper as he was dying that he was going to write about focusing on living. We need to return to living, striving, and seeking in the everyday world. We need to live in two worlds, the inner and the outer, while developing a new vision of who we are and our unique purpose for being here.

The experience in the Temple and on the road back always includes an increased need for self-expression. In this part of the journey, we have become immersed in life, a life we have feared and in some way longed for. We have journeyed into life, into consciousness, into reality, and into meaning. It is important now to find ways to express our experiences, whether it is through writing, painting, dancing, quilting, hiking, or simply listening to and being with others on similar journeys.

As we go out of ourselves, we continue to be re-creating ourselves. Our life is unique and needs to be expressed in some form to be truly lived. Another function of the return is to learn how to express the love and support we have experienced from our big Self in the way we love life and relate to other people. Too often in psychology, we only focus on the love that we didn't receive when we were small and needed it, or on the perverted love that wounded us. These wounds need to be healed, or they can make us sick. However, we also need to focus on how we can develop our own unique ways of expressing love and realizing that love opens barriers within and without of ourselves. Love heals, as we know, yet we are afraid to face this knowledge because we have been taught so many silly and inappropriate self-sacrificing ideas about love.

Part of our Return is to bring love back to its rightful place as our highest spiritual value. Unless we are well on the path to self-knowledge, love remains a part of our unconscious life, full of unresolved, unacknowledged fantasies, ideals, needs, and hurts. Love without insight and understanding lacks form and direction. Sentimental love, for example, robs us of strength, certainty, and purpose. Romantic love becomes obsessive or compulsive. What we think of as love may actually be an idealistic fantasy or the longing for security and emotional healing. When it is all said and done, our early wounds, if unhealed, can make us sick, and the wounds that keep us from feeling and expressing love are just as vital to our healing and wholeness. Self-knowledge is the indispensable ingredient for authentic love to heal and enrich our lives. It is only through our sublime moments of experiencing love that we can bring the beauty of it into our full awareness—even in the midst of our discouragement and pain, even in a hospital or hospice room.

Thoughts and Questions to Ponder...

What are your feelings and reflections about what I shared about grief in this chapter?

But once I and the other people I've worked with accepted that this change is inevitable, and that we must listen to what our bodies, our illnesses, and our big Self are trying to tell us, then a path appeared. Grief for the passing of an old self, of our old life and personality, is necessary. But grief is tricky. It must be experienced fully, but we must not get caught or bogged down in it. We must give it its due and then choose life.

What do you feel about what I shared in this passage?

While we are in the Temple, we realize that no matter how much we want to be the person we used to be, it is not going to happen. But if we are devoted to this path, we also discover we are not alone. We have the history of human experience that we are becoming part of, and we have the hidden hands that can support us, that can rise up from our big Self, if we seek them and are open to them.

What are your thoughts about each of the truths that I shared with you that I feel are so important:

First, I have learned that the fundamental assertion in most mystical traditions—that self-knowledge is the way to come to know the Divine—is absolutely true. Self-knowledge releases us from the prison of our personal history, deconditions us from the attitudes of our parents and society, and forces us to work through our losses, hurts, and grief. This act of purification, as the mystics called it, opens us to our depths, to the Self, the Divine energy within us.

The second truth I realized is that compassion must begin with myself...

Self-love anchored in self-knowledge is the underpinning of how well we can give and receive love. Without self-love, our structure of relationships will crumble under the pressure of the smallest storms, and our so-called unselfish acts will create an inner cauldron of resentment.

161

The third thing I discovered is that a life based on the pursuit of self-knowledge continually takes us back into the world and among our communities. We cannot live a wholehearted life alone. We must participate in all the various relationships—attractions, love, friendships, conflicts, projections—to gain stimulation as well as the content that informs much of our search for self-knowledge.

The fourth and final thing that I gradually became aware of is that something inside me cares about me and my life. If I listen, it speaks to me through my dreams, fantasies, inspiration, and thoughts. When I reflect, journal, and work with my active imagination, it helps heal my wounds, turns my symptoms and failures into lessons, and aids me in discerning what my soul wants for my life. It does not save me from any of life's difficulties or catastrophes. But when I am suffering, it is there with me.

Other thoughts…

CHAPTER 19

Our Own Love Story: Choosing Life

Blessed by all things,
Wings of breath,
Delight of eyes,
Wonder of whisper,
Intimacy of touch,
Eternity of soul.

– JOHN O'DONOHUE

Listening to music that touches, inspires, and calms me is an important part of my life and healing. I sit quietly, listen, and seek to center myself. I know that when we think about it, between you and me, we know that when we are sick, we want to get well. We don't want to change our personalities, face our bad habits, change our attitudes, or consider that much of our approach to life has been on the wrong track and that we may need to start again from a place of new awareness.

One of my favorite pieces of music is written and performed by Rabbi David Zeller, the son of one of the first Jungian analysts in America. The title of this album is *Ruach*. As many of you know, this is the Hebrew word for spirit. The spirit is the power that supports a deeper voice within us that calls us to healing and wholeness, a voice that calls us beyond getting well but that can easily be drowned out by our fear and loneliness. Deep in our heart, our greatest fear is that we may lose our identity or be stripped of it. And we fear that we may not be recognized, valued, heard, or have our own voice. But the inner voice of the spirit is an even deeper voice in our heart, calling us to healing, to a homecoming, to a rebirth into our true, authentic, and complete selves. Remember that radical hope and this path are born out of love and are supported by a love story woven through the centuries of human nature—a love story with life. Ultimately the quest of individuation is a love story because it leads us beyond the opposites of health and illness into a love of life.

Credit: Jörg Bittner Unna

Figure 23. Michelangelo's sculpture

In the quest, we become an artist participating with the Divine, the Self, in creating our lives, sculpting them from the raw marble of our biology and our heritage, into the unique pattern of our potential that wants to emerge into the world just as Michelangelo's figures struggle to emerge from marble. And at this point, we have clearly entered the temple of Asclepius.

We have left the realm of Hippocratic medicine, where we see our bodies mechanically. I have no criticism for this perspective, for it is powerful, useful, and we must not abandon it. But we must also learn the perspective of Asclepius, the god of healing. This perspective takes us into the symbolic life, where life and our bodies are seen symbolically and as metaphors. If we choose the quest and answer the call, we are actually choosing life, and then our life becomes a love story. We must keep this reality foremost in our daily vision of living as we learn to face the horror and the beauty that we will experience.

Our Love Story Must Begin with Self-Love

Self-love, in its fullest sense, becomes a burning necessity for us to affirm once we have begun to open ourselves to our wholeness. Only the return of the Master, the deeper aspects of ourselves, can open us to life as a love story. This love story begins with loving ourselves, forgiving ourselves, and allowing our big Self to welcome us home so we can embody the love in the center of our being.

Credit: Science Museum, London, Wellcome Images

Figure 24. Model of the Asklepion at Epidaurus, Greece, 1936

Here are the seven principles that I have used in my lectures and writings that are necessary to open the door to self-love one day at a time:

1. Remember, love is difficult, the poet Rilke explains, in contrast to the sentimental way we like to think about it. Review your thoughts about love. Do you think it should just bring happiness, ease, or at least security? Do explosions, struggles, and failure make you think love has failed? Life isn't easy, and love can't be easy either.

2. Cultivating self-love is an odyssey with moments of difficulty and joy. It's an excursion into knowing ourselves, into asking whether what we are doing is adding to or diminishing how we feel about ourselves.

3. Self-love challenges the boundaries of how we have fenced ourselves into practicality, conventional wisdom, and other people's perspectives. We must gently ask ourselves, whose voice are we really hearing in our head? Is it the voice of our heart or of our true Self?

4. Self-love isn't self-indulgent. It isn't shopping sprees, outlandish vacations, sneaking sweets, or pouting moods. It is the commitment to growing in self-knowledge and our capacity to love. Remember, taking the time for reflection isn't egocentric. It is the key to having the kind of vitality that overflows.

5. Self-love is the foundation that determines how strongly we can give and receive love. Without it, our relationships will crumble under the slightest storm. Take the responsibility for understanding your fears and needs, and for facing them in a loving way.

6. Self-love rests on self-forgiveness, on being able to understand who we were when we failed ourselves, and what needs, hurts, fears, and deprivations were driving us. Only then may we meet ourselves with compassion and kindness. This is why our growth in self-understanding brings healing and reconciliation with our essential selves.

7. Self-love is learning how to be tough with ourselves and to take the driver's seat in our life when we need to break a destructive mood or habit. We must remember that being tough with ourselves means being committed and energetic, having high standards and tenacity. Being tough with ourselves is the opposite of being hard on ourselves, which means being perfectionistic, self-critical, self-punishing, and unaccepting of our mistakes and weaknesses. It is important for us to remember each day that to embody love, to be love, begins with a foundation of self-love and self-compassion every day.

Love Requires Courage—But What Is That?

As the emissary has taken over our lives, the meaning of another of our noblest qualities—courage—has lost the depth of its meaning. On this journey that we have been thrust into—for it to become a quest, we must have the courage to learn and seek. And even if we become seekers out of desperation, it still takes courage, because it is easy to fall into despair, bitterness, and hopelessness in the face of our illness.

Courage is the ability to look our fears in the face—even our greatest fears—as we did in the Temple when facing the burning bush. Then we must go ahead doing what the inner quest has taught us—that we remember what we value the most, what is right for our lives. By doing what is right for our lives, we contribute to all life.

Courage is to look into the abyss of the darkness in our lives, in ourselves, and to search for meaning, new purpose, new directions, and the path to grow beyond our small selves. This idea is one of Dr. Jung's greatest contributions: the understanding that we are being called by our symptoms, illnesses, and struggles to heal, to become whole, and to grow beyond our difficulties into new, stronger, broader versions of who we are. When we love ourselves, when we feel the love and support of our center—our big Self—we find the courage and the energy to imagine new things, new lives. The experience of being loved creates in us the desire to be transformed.

Facing Our Horror and Beauty

In her earlier dialog with a dream figure that told Beth she was the real Beth, Beth came face to face with her shadow, that part of her, both good and bad, that contains her unlived life. This authentic figure surprised and confronted Beth with how closed and encaged her personality was in her ideas of who she was.

I'm no stranger to this condition. I have a strong ego and have often discovered that I was in a strong cage, even when I was considering myself very open. Like Beth, my dreams and my illnesses confronted me. When our unlived life shows up and breaks in, we are often shocked by the power

Figure 25. Woman in a cage

169

of its entry. The more unknown and uncanny and unacknowledged this life force is, the more likely it is to strike the body, sometimes causing a very serious illness. Then, then our illness becomes the path to wholeness and a fully lived life.

I have often found that when we become sick, it is because we cannot go forward with a needed development. You may recall that Dr. Jung was seriously ill before he wrote *God's Answer to Job* because he was so resistant to accepting the ideas and emotions that his psyche was pushing him to encounter. In cases like this, our illness can become the path to new growth and to the energy that needs to come into our consciousness and be actualized. Then, if we can take it in and intentionally live it, there will be a restructuring and rebirthing of our personality.

Of course, following this counter-rational path toward healing and wholeness is not easy. It is hard, yet it is worth the effort. All that immediate material we have to confront, the unaccepted, unassimilated, and unlived life, is difficult and often disturbing to discover and confront. It may also bring great relief and renewed hope. And while at first it may seem beyond our endurance, this is where we have to start. I believe that it helps us endure it if we have a map of the journey and the knowledge that others have traveled this way.

Thoughts and Questions to Ponder…

This chapter is about love and about courage, and looking at these attributes in new ways. Take time to digest each of these passages, and then express your feelings about them.

Only the tapping into and the return of the deeper aspects of ourselves can open us to life as a love story. This love story begins with loving ourselves, forgiving ourselves, and allowing our big Self to welcome us home so we can embody the love in the center of our being.

Courage is the ability to look our fears in the face—even our greatest fears—as we did in the Temple when facing the burning bush. Then we must go ahead, doing what the inner quest has taught us that we value the most, what is right for our lives—and by doing what is right for our lives, contributing to all life.

When we love ourselves, when we feel the love and support of our center—our big Self—we find the courage and the energy to imagine new things, new lives. The experience of being loved creates in us the desire to be transformed.

Courage is to look into the abyss of the darkness in our lives, in ourselves, and to search for meaning, new purpose, new directions, and the path to grow beyond our small selves.

As I mentioned, listening to music that touches, inspires, and calms me is an important part of my life and healing. I sit quietly, listen, and seek to center myself. What ways have you found in your life that help calm you and help you get to center yourself?

Other thoughts…

CHAPTER 20

A Sacred Journey: The Art of Self-Creation

May you be granted the courage and vision
To work through passivity and self-pity,
To see the beauty you can harvest
From the riches of this dark invitation.

— JOHN O'DONOHUE

To make our lives into a sacred journey—as our quest is now becoming—requires, as all spiritual growth does, methodical devotion. If we want a life of healing, wholeness, meaning, fulfillment, joy, love, and purpose, we have to pay close attention to it. This is what Dr. Jung referred to as paying "religious attention" to it. These are the fruits of self-knowledge and spiritual development that cannot be obtained in any other way.

As Tom Swift, I, and many others have realized, our illness may actually be our impetus that compels this journey. Whatever illusion we have distracted ourselves with up to now, whether it is busyness, obligations, or positive thinking, being a pleaser, achiever, or whatever, it has simply been a means of sleepwalking through or avoiding the facing our lives.

If, however, we begin to keep a journal, write down our dreams, and do active imagination, several interesting things will happen: we will begin to think in terms of reflecting on our lives or losing them. Just the act of "being there" for our soul, our big Self, becomes powerful and life enhancing. The more we examine our lives, the more natural it becomes to see the world in symbolic terms and to realize that the capacity for symbolic vision is the foundation of developing healing and wholeness. It is the foundation for returning the Master to his or her natural place in our lives. We are then led to realize that paying attention is the acid test of love, and we must love ourselves and life in this most important way.

In the film about the life and works of Dr. Jung, *A Matter of Heart*, Sir Laurens van der Post, a Jungian scholar who was also a friend and biographer of Dr. Jung's, explains a very important point in Dr. Jung's thinking. This point is that if we live our life religiously (meaning by paying careful attention to it) and symbolically, then it becomes sacred. Sir Laurens explained that it becomes almost as if what the theologians call "God" and the native Africans call "the first spirit" has passed over some key responsibilities to the human being, and the human being had a God-like task to perform in creation. To the extent to which we perform the task—in growing into wholeness—we derive our meaning. This is what can happen to us when we undertake this journey into our healing and wholeness, and the inner quest of seeking our greater Self.

Self-knowledge brings our greatest healing, as it links our mind, body, emotions, and spirit into a focused whole. Through this journey into facing the darkness in our lives, the challenge of our illness, and the deeper needs of healing within us, we discover the course of our lives, our greater Self, and the Divine within us that infuses our body, mind, and heart with life, love, and creative power, and allows us to understand the underlying notion of wholeness that the great religions all speak of.

Once we are on the journey and are entering *The Phase of the Return*, the next question is, "How can we approach the task of renewing our symbolic life?" We must face our own inner work as a sacred journey rather than as a series of activities, treatments, tasks, or exercises. We must pull over from how we have been driving through life and stop in order to develop the art of living.

We don't have to reflect for very long to realize that our daily emphasis on rationality and functionality has impoverished our ability to see life with wonder and meaning. It has also exhausted our capacity to have real respect for the great dramas of life's passages, for the continuous need for initiations that truly help us transition from an old perspective on life to a new one. It dims our capacity to understand that an illness is calling for us to create a healing environment within ourselves to bring about transformation.

In my experience, our ability to face life's challenges, to die to an old version of who we have been, to be reborn into a new and greater version of ourselves, to live more fully, and to help transform the world around us is truly a *miracle*. As we learn to exchange the old external authorities around us, with their rules and expectations that we had internalized…for our own inner authority, our imagination comes to play a major role in our healing and growth. Our imagination becomes the ground of our new visions of our selves and of life and the meeting place for our small self and our big Self. The meeting of our small self and our big Self generates the energy for change and taps the life force within us, and our imagination then becomes a vehicle for transformation, inviting us into a life of new meaning and potentials.

Our first step in cultivating the art of living is to learn to truly value our imagination, and to value it means to give it time and attention. In addition, if it is going to become life renewing and transformative, we must realize that it is creative and sacred. And of course, if it is creative, it is also art and in this case becomes the field or context within which the art of self-creation begins. As a result, it is also our personal source of culture and re-creation. Re-creation begins with reflecting carefully upon our experiences of life. It also includes our devotion to practices that give our reflections and imagination a "temenos" or sacred space in our lives.

You may recall that Beth created a special space and atmosphere, almost like an altar in her room, where she did her inner work. Creating such a space is where we can invite our unconscious to participate in our lives. If I can imagine a witch in a fairy tale in this space as picturing a part of myself, I am on the way to being open to dialoging with my illness, my cancer cells, my lesions, or other symptoms. Through my imagination, I can contact the consciousness in my body. And I should also remember that if it gets too threatening, I can say, "Stop, that is enough." Then I should take this work to a therapist or analyst.

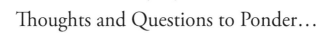

Thoughts and Questions to Ponder...

The first step in cultivating the art of self-creation is to learn to truly value our imagination and to give it time and attention.

Imagination is creative and sacred.

Imagination is art.

Imagination is the context within
which the art of self-creation begins.

Imagination is evidence of the Divine.

Imagination needs a sacred place and attitude in order to invite our whole self, including our unconscious, to participate in our lives.

What are you feelings and experiences about this level of Imagination?

How do you take time to cultivate your Imagination?

From my book *Sacred Selfishness*:

"Our imaginations are the spaces, the fields, where our conscious personalities and the many parts of our unconscious can meet each other, struggle, play, dream, and transform us."

Our everyday self and the outer world have become split from our unconscious and the inner world. Our Imagination can mediate between them.

The Imaginative space is where our conscious and unconscious can meet...where our small self can meet in an interactive field with our complexes, dream figures, physical and psychic symptoms, strong emotions, illnesses, our deepest desires, and figures that emerge from our unconscious in active imagination.

How do you feel that the Imaginative space could be helpful to you in your journey "beyond normal"?

As I mentioned, when we face a dramatic diagnosis, one of our greatest fears is that we may lose our identity or be stripped of it.

And we fear that we may not be recognized, valued, or heard, or have our own voice, our own dignity, and our own vision of life.

Both Dr. Jung and Dr. Frankl agreed that the will to meaning is part of our nature and necessary to our health, fulfillment, and survival.

Meaning is not just a matter of success and happiness but also a matter of fulfillment and survival. Dr. Jung said that we can endure almost anything if we can understand its meaning.

It is important to go deep into our true nature to discover a sense of meaning in your illness and suffering. This is exercising the most creative of all human potentials.

For you, how will finding a sense of meaning in your illness and suffering help you tap into radical hope?

Other thoughts…

CHAPTER 21

Proper Questions to Ask

May my mind come alive today
To the invisible geography
That invites me to new frontiers,
To break the dead shell of yesterdays,
To risk being disturbed and changed.

— John O'Donohue

One of the hardest lessons I've had to learn in my life is that myths and fairy tales are true. For example, for most of my life, I loved the King Arthur stories. Then at one point, I began to quit enjoying the story of Parsifal and his quest for the Holy Grail.

Figure 26. Parsifal Holding the Grail

I soon realized that Parsifal's quest was not an intentional journey of self-actualization. His journey began in the face of disaster and failure. The conventional life that, in fact, King Arthur had achieved had become a wasteland, and Parsifal's quest was a desperate search for healing. So was mine.

The Holy Grail is the symbolic container of the healing powers deep within us, and all those years ago, I had little knowledge of what that meant. Of course, Parsifal didn't know what it meant either, and that is why his quest began with failure. When he first encountered the Grail, he was not prepared for the encounter by conventional wisdom, values, his success as a knight, nor by practical advice, and he didn't know the right questions to ask of the Grail. The Grail then disappeared, and his first encounter ended as a miserable and confusing failure. But he persisted, and I learned to persist.

Like Parsifal, I learned that it took a long and committed quest to gain enough life experience and wisdom learned from suffering and struggle to give up trying to be in control of my life and to be humble enough to ask the Grail the proper questions—the questions that would open its healing powers. These are the same questions I ask my shadow, my dream figures, and most of all my symptoms and my illnesses—and they are:

1. **"What ails thee?"** or **"What is troubling you?"** This Grail question needs to come from the depth of our compassion—a compassion that can only come from our acceptance of our own pain and failures. If I am asking this of a symptom or illness, it is because I know that it is important and not just some unfortunate or evil event to be overcome or defeated. It is part of me, and I must honor it, even if that part is meant to die.

2. The second question comes from other Grail stories and is, **"How can I help?"** This is the question that allows our illness to confront us with how we need to change our lives and what we need to face about ourselves in order to discover how we can help ourselves by helping it. This question required that I be courageous and humble, and that I had learned that humility and despair are very different. Humility accepts reality and helplessness, while despair is often over our lack of power and control and the failure of our expectations.

3. The third question from Grail stories is, **"Whom does the Grail serve?"** or **"What purpose do my symptoms or illness serve?"** The answer to this question in the story is that the Grail serves the servers of the Grail. This question means that if the Grail, the source of life and healing within us, can help us, then we too must learn to serve it. In other words, we must learn from our illness.

Figure 27. Person Breaking out of the Egg

The result of answering these questions means that we are breaking out of our old goals, values, and ideas of a good life and have the capacity to see life anew, to live differently…from our center with a deeper understanding of love, and that we will rejoin the world in making our unique contributions to it. In summary, I would say that if I am open and able to ask my symptoms, illnesses, shadow, and dream figures the first two questions—"What ails thee?" and "How can I help?"—the third question will begin to be answered.

Love Heals

Love is the most powerful healing and integrating force on Earth. As you will see in the following dialog by Beth, as she uses the Grail questions, it takes a strong commitment and a long journey into self-knowledge to face what it really means to love and nurture ourselves. In the next few dialogs by Gail, you can see that to discover the wellspring of love within us also takes a lot of self-knowledge and the willingness to open ourselves to the healing force of wholeness within us. It also takes a desire to align ourselves with the love deep within us…the love that is the power that sustains and transforms life everywhere.

Asking the Grail questions aligns us with the great archetypal feminine principles of receptivity, nurturance and transformation that are an essential, though often unrecognized, part of who we are. When we are able to ask these questions and take this stance, then we are capable of listening to our bodies, our illnesses, our shadows and other rejected parts of ourselves with compassion.

Most of us know from our own experiences that when someone has compassion for us, we find ourselves really seen, heard and attended to. If such a person is willing to speak, act and even suffer with us and for us, they mark our lives…we never forget them. So it is vitally important for us to learn how to respond to ourselves in this compassionate way that is profoundly human and puts us in touch with the Divine.

Beth learned more about what it meant to face the challenge and the deep need to love herself and to begin to heal the inner wasteland that her illness revealed to her, as she began asking her lesions the Grail questions…

> **Beth:** Well, Lesions, we've gotten to know each other a bit and you've shaken me up pretty good. Now I want to ask you, "What is troubling you?"
>
> **Lesions:** We're glad you are asking. Our main problem is how you have separated yourself from your body, long before we came along. Your body, including us, is filled with hostility and resentment because you have pushed so much self-animosity into it and then tried to imprison it there. You have been pushing your

emotions into your body and pushing the pain they cause in your body away.

The way we are split is what's troubling us.

Beth: Damn! I knew this was going to be hard. Just listening to you is exhausting. But I won't quit. Let's keep going. How can I help?

Lesions: You have to learn that being split is a way of coping that goes back longer than you can remember. Being split also caused you to become selective in denial of a scary, painful reality. But being split between your mind and emotions/body is like a double bind.

The body feels that you and your emotions are against it. The more you fight to contain the feelings you buried for decades, the more your body feels attacked.

Then more tension, discomfort and pain develops. You are actually still using this style of coping in your present day conflicts. Your pain and your legs are crying out for attention, for love, for understanding.

Beth: You are saying too much, too many things and I am trying to hear you. But my childhood wasn't all bad. I was cared for, and even loved. We had a lot of good times, too.

Lesions: I know that, but you didn't live in a climate of safety. You always felt on guard, vulnerable. And there were many times when you were hurt, lonely and never felt really listened to and understood. You also blamed yourself at a deep level for not being "good enough."

Beth: Okay, that may be true. Anyways, how can I help?

Lesions: To have a true love for yourself, you must first have a true appreciation for what you went through. All of the hidden things—the events, feelings, reactions and fears—are continuing to haunt you, to affect your health. All these buried things are alive, and your past is lying heavily upon you.

Beth: I know I have to realize and accept all of this, but is there room for a remedy? Is there a way I can help?

Lesions: You must key into the old dreaded feelings, let them out of their prison and greet them with love and compassion. Let the pain in your legs begin to tell you about the fear and loneliness that little Beth felt—and that you still feel today. Let your bladder tell you how tired it is of always trying to hold things in. Let your fatigue tell you how tired you are of not being able to confront people. Let it tell you how afraid little Beth was, and is, to speak up and out about the things that matter deeply and personally. Let them all carry you back to your roots so you can see how the pain-producing patterns grew over the years.

Beth: Oh, God! You are direct, to say the least. But is that all?

Lesions: Not even close. I'm speaking for your body.

I haven't ever really been heard before and now I want to say as much as I can. But I don't want to scare you out of talking to me.

Beth: I'm scared, but now I am determined to continue talking with you and I will not quit.

Lesions: Practice listening. Keep asking these Grail questions. Practice loving yourself. Massage your legs as if you want to give them love and use healing oils every day. Tell them how much you appreciate how they have carried you through life. Tell them how sorry you are for their pain that you tried to chase away and not pay attention to; but that now you are listening to. Be grateful for your own fighting spirit and learn to use it to support loving yourself in all circumstances. Remember that true self-love grows a step at a time, and true healing bit by bit.

Beth: I am a bit overwhelmed. I don't know what to say. I'm going to need some time to absorb all of this. But, thank you.

Beth was amazed at what the lesions were saying and so was I. She kept dialoging with them and with her legs, getting them to help her unwind the stories and the history of the events and feelings trapped there. During this process her inner relationship with herself was growing and so was her internal sense of becoming more at home within herself. The more her body came to be accepted and loved, the more healing changes became possible for her. Beth began seeing new potentials for healing, for inner freedom and for love.

We live in a society that talks about love all the time, but in reality there are very few models that help us learn how to love ourselves and each other in a genuine way. I offer help for this journey in my book, *Sacred Selfishness: A Guide to Living a Life of Substance* and in the book by my wife, Massimilla Harris and me, *Into the Heart of the Feminine: Facing the Death Mother Archetype to Reclaim Love, Strength and Vitality.*

◆ ◆ ◆

In our next dialog, Gail is beginning her conversation with her immune system. Over two decades ago, she went through a far-reaching healing process with breast cancer. Today she has been facing several auto-immune problems which include painful reoccurring experiences of shingles. Her dialogs may seem short, but they were very intense for her and took place over several days. These are her dialogs.

Day One

> **Gail:** I would like to speak to my immune system or a representative. I have had shingles four times since May, and pneumonia, urinary tract infection and painful mouth ulcers. Yes, I have been under a great deal of stress with ending of my marriage. But I think this goes even deeper than all of the above. Would a representative step forward to help me by answering some questions?
>
> **Immune System:** Yes, I am the representative stepping forward. My name is Left Behind. I will be the one who represents the entire immune system, for the system is wide and deep.
>
> **Gail:** Thanks, Left Behind. Thanks for being the representative and being willing to talk with me. First I sincerely want to thank you and the entire immune system for taking such good care of me for 72+ years. Over the years there has been a lot of toxicity in my body. Thank you for keeping me safe and healthy with, at times, an overwhelming amount of toxicity.

Left Behind: You are welcome and thank you for acknowledging our help. Now what is on your mind?

Gail: I'm just wondering if you can share with me what has been troubling you all these years? I ask what is troubling you because you seem to be struggling to fight infections. I know I contribute when I am overloaded with stress, but is this more than stress?

Left Behind: Stress is a major player in our system, but this goes deeper than stress. As you already know, this troubling cause goes to the blood stream and deeper to where the antibodies are made. Actually, you inherited this disorder from your mother and you passed it on to your son. All that is talk about the organics and biology of us, immune system.

Gail: Yes, I know but I want to know what is going on deep within you and me. What troubles you, Left Behind?

Left Behind: First, let me say, I was left behind when you were being formed in your mother. Your mother was only concerned about herself, so she used as many of the bodily parts as possible for herself. I, as a developing cell, was left behind with no way to protect myself or grow and develop.

So you needed immunity but there wasn't much because your mother was taking everything for herself. Really your mother only wanted to catch your dad, any way possible. She wanted him for her own pleasure and desire. She didn't care about us, me and you. That might be hard to understand but, in simple terms, she was only about herself. She didn't really care about you or me as being important. Remember she wanted your dad for herself alone. She was never sure that was going to work cause she was unsure if he really loved her. But to tell the truth, he didn't know how to love either or care about her.

Gail: Okay, I have to take a break for a bit. This is a little too much for right now.

186

Day Two

Gail: I'm back for more conversation, Left Behind. Where did you get your name and what does it mean?

Left Behind: That's a long story, but here goes. When a being is developing, all parts are needed. That's just basic biology. But a feeling of deep down love and caring is also needed. I am that deep down loving caring part of you who was left behind in those early years. I felt like I had been ignored, overlooked, not important. I am love in the purest form, Gail. I came from the universe from all there is, so to speak. I had lots of love to give to you, but I was not included in your development. So I took the name Left Behind. I am the left behind love and compassion that the giver of all things gives each being. But I did not have a place in your becoming cause I was left behind. Maybe a better way of expressing is to say, Left Out. All beings need an immune system to keep the body working well and for fighting illnesses and harmful things that get in and make a being sick. But there is more to that system—like love, compassion, acceptance, caring, unconditional love and acceptance. That's what I'm made of—all those things make me. And I, we, were left out, left behind. Oh, we've always been present, waiting to be invited back in, but no one noticed or invited us to be a part of the immune system and to be a part of you.

Day Three

Gail: Dear Left Out/Left Behind, how is the best way to invite you back in to my immune system? By the way, I learned from going to the doctor that there is nothing biologically wrong with my immune system. All the stress I have experienced this year has caused the problems. And, I suspect all the qualities you have to give me were not there, which also caused problems.

Left Behind: Yes, the doctor confirmed what I'm saying that there is more to the immune system than biology. Love, compassion, acceptance, loving kindness are so, so important. I am going to sum everything up by using the word LOVE. You did not receive the deep down pure LOVE you needed as you were developing.

Now your question is how can love be invited back in? I and we (immune system parts) are pure LOVE. We were there twenty-three years ago to help you through breast cancer. And we were absent when you developed breast cancer. You did not invite us back in then, but we knew you needed us badly. Now today, you are at a new turning point, and you have suffered so much for seventy-two years without all of us being with you totally. We care about you deeply and love you for eternity. You have been looking for LOVE and all of us forever.

Gail: Yes, yes. I know because I have yearned to be loved, to know LOVE but you have not been present fully. Please tell me how I can invite you back in to my life.

Left Behind: It is simple, really. Open your heart, remember when you were at the retreat center years ago and John brought you a bowl of healing soup. Remember when you opened the door and said, "Is this for me?" He said, "Yes, I brought this for you." Remember how your heart opened at that moment? You opened yourself to receive the soup which was given in love to you.

You dropped all the barriers around your heart and received. So once again, it is that simple. Open your heart for all of us to come in. God created you with love, you have always been loved and always will be loved. The big question for you is, "Can you allow yourself to receive LOVE?"

Gail: I want to say yes, but I'm not sure at this moment.

Left Behind: Well, take your time while you let all of what we've said sink in. And, by the way, LOVE is not the same thing as being nice or trying to make other people feel good, or smiling and being pleasant. LOVE is more than pleasant feelings. LOVE can be difficult and full of struggles. LOVE is not about performing. LOVE is about accepting yourself—all the parts of yourself.

In the inner work you've done over the years, you've discovered lots of forgotten parts, shadow parts, parts that have been discounted or denied, and we are saying all those parts are LOVE. And just as LOVE can be difficult and full of struggles, LOVE can be full of wonder, imagination, zest for living. Pure, real LOVE is all parts, all sides. And it's not about being perfect!!!! It is about being REAL, a real person or being, like the Velveteen Rabbit. Remember this rabbit was so full of love and had received and given so much love, that he was worn down almost to threads. He was about to be forgotten and thrown away when a magic fairy turned him into a real bunny.

So can you be real, Gail? Not the pretend nice Gail. And can you open your heart to yourself? Nothing else matters. Only you can open your heart. Can you open your heart and let the light in? It is all up to you. We want to come back in and always be with you. But you are the one who must open her heart so we can come in.

Gail: And the reality is for most of my life, if not all of it, life has been filled with fear—fear of not being worthy or good enough, fear I was always alone and would forever be alone. Fear, fear, of never knowing LOVE has kept me trapped. I need lots of guidance, strength and courage to step out…into LOVE.

Left Behind: Nothing to fear, Gail. This is a life-long process and journey. You set your intention now and remind yourself every day. So we suggest you stay in touch with yourself and LOVE within by writing in your journal, being grateful and staying conscious. Of course, be conscious of our dreams. Remember we all are with you because you have opened your heart and invited us in. Plus, you can talk to us anytime.

Gail: Thank you so much. Oh, by the way, can I ask another question?

Left Behind: Of course, what is your question?

Gail: During those stressful days, why the shingles?

Left Behind: The shingles originated long ago in childhood as chicken pox, and we thought shingles was a good attention getter and reminder of not knowing you were loved. We were trying to get your attention to the pure LOVE always being there.

◆ ◆ ◆

As you read and reflect on these dialogs, remember the third Grail question, "Whom does the Grail serve?" or "What purpose do my symptoms or illness serve?"

What do you imagine the answer to these questions would be for Beth and Gail based on these two dialogs?

Thoughts and Questions to Ponder...

The Grail Questions

We spoke about the grail legend...

Parsifal, a knight in the King Arthur story, was searching for the Holy Grail to heal the tragedy that had fallen on the kingdom and had turned it into a wasteland. By becoming a knight, he had fulfilled his boyhood ambitions and became an outstanding success. But this had not prepared him for the quest for healing. And when he first encountered the Holy Grail—the potentials for new life and healing—he didn't know the right questions to ask. He failed. However, he did not give up but was committed to the quest while suffering, struggling, and learning.

What do we need to learn from the legendary story of Parsifal and his quest for the Holy Grail—the source of healing renewal and transformation—needed for the wasteland that King Arthur's kingdom had become? How can this story benefit us on our healing journey to a place beyond normal? Like Parsifal, I learned that it took a long and committed quest to gain enough life experience and wisdom, learned from suffering and struggle, to give up trying to be in control of my life and be humble enough to ask the Grail the proper questions—the questions that would open its healing powers.

The Holy Grail is the symbolic container of the healing powers deep within us.

Now it is time to ask yourself at your own soul level these Grail questions:

What ails thee? What is troubling you at a core level?

Ask yourself this question with compassion.

In silence, breathe deeply for a few minutes.

How can I help?

This question to the Grail permits our illness to confront us with how we need to change and what we need to face.

Whom does the Grail serve?

We come to learn that the Grail or source of life can help us…and that we can serve the source of life.

How are these ideas of the healing power of illness affecting you?

What feelings are coming up in you?

Are you surprised in any way?

Other thoughts…

CHAPTER 22

The Healing Wisdom of Dreams

I bless the night that nourished my heart
To set the ghosts of longing free
Into the flow and figure of dream
That went to harvest from the dark
Bread for the hunger no one sees.

— John O'Donohue

In these next chapters, we are going to talk about the art of living. In developing the art of living, we recover the value of living through reflection, rituals, symbols, and our unconscious. We build an inner life that can give meaning to our experiences, a life where the engagement with our joys and suffering, our successes and failures, renews us and inspires us to grow.

I first got the idea of "befriending my dreams" over forty years ago from the Jungian analyst and author Dr. James Hillman. In his book *The Dream and the Underworld*, Dr. Hillman challenged us to "re-vision" how we had learned to work with dreams. He claimed that our dreams have been colonized by rational, ego-based schools of psychology and other approaches, which have devalued, betrayed, and destroyed their more profound symbolic messages.

Modern psychology and some modern approaches to dreams that claim to be Jungian have, in Dr. Hillman's perspective and in mine too, committed the twin crimes of imperialism and genocide when it comes to the meaning in our dreams. Dr. Hillman says, "Each morning we repeat western history, slaying our brother, the dream, by killing its images with interpretative concepts that explain the dream to the ego. Ego, over black coffee (a ritual of sympathetic magic), chases the shadows of the night and reinforces his domain."

I followed Dr. Hillman's ideas as I shared my approach to honoring my dreams in my book *Sacred Selfishness: A Guide to Living a Life of*

Substance. I am going to share my thoughts about treating our dreams as friends in that book with you.

From *Sacred Selfishness: A Guide to Living a Life of Substance*, pp. 224-229:

Dreams as Friends

True friendship is both an art and a craft. Friendships may often seem to begin easily, but their nature is delicate at first, growth is slow and is easily checked or diverted. For friendships to become strong they need to be nurtured, cultivated, and appreciated. Few of us are born with a natural gift for cultivating friendships. They take time, caring, and mutual respect. And the busyness that devours our lives makes enriching our friendships difficult. But once a friendship has become strong, it's very sturdy and reliable. A real friend can tell us things we don't want to tell ourselves and yet we're always comforted to know there's someone out there we can lean on.

Some years ago writer Sophie Loeb said, "A friend is one who withholds judgment no matter how long you have his unanswered letter." These characteristics of friendships explain why befriending the dream is an idea that makes immediate sense to most of us. It's much more comforting to feel that our inner lives are friendly toward us even if they're provoking us with dramatic images or confronting our preferred opinions.

In therapy it's tempting for both the therapist and the patient to translate dreams into their favorite theories, perspectives, or rationalizations. In many of these situations, dream interpretations are used to dredge up childhood conflicts; or to gain information, power, or energy from our unconscious to help us pursue our goals. Yet these approaches are actually hostile to our unconscious. They go against the grain of friendships for nothing damages a friendship more than trying to exploit it. Unfortunately, modern therapies are often influenced by the social character of our times, which emphasizes solving problems in order to become more functional, rather than honoring our inner lives so that we can become more whole as human beings. When the fruits of friendship and the cultivation of our inner lives and wisdom aren't valued, therapy can actually work against our healing and growth and contribute to devaluing life.

The beauty of befriending dreams is that it doesn't require special knowledge and training. It simply asks that we listen to what they have to say to us and appreciate their importance.

Paying Attention

Paying attention to our dream lives involves several activities. To begin with it's beneficial if we can create favorable conditions for receiving our dreams. An overextended schedule, exhaustion, poor sleeping habits, and the general habit of just being too busy can distract us from the quality time we commit to our dreams, or for that matter to any friendship. Making an effort to create an attitude of interest and receptivity by trying to have a good night's sleep and waking up gently very likely will invite a response from our unconscious.

The second way of paying attention to dreams is to write them down as soon as we wake up. It's better not to put them off till morning if we remember them in the middle of the night, or to wait until after we've had coffee and are dressed. Time and experience have proven that until this friendship is firmly established, no matter how often we go over a dream in our minds, we can lose it in a moment if we haven't written it down.

Research proves we dream every night. If we don't remember their contents it usually means we're overtired, anxious, or haven't been interested in or have some other trouble keeping us from concentrating on our inner lives. Having a pencil and paper available nearby and writing dreams down quickly is a helpful ritual that stimulates our memory of them. When we wake up and don't remember a dream, lying quietly and focusing on what we have been thinking since we awakened can be helpful. Perhaps a thought or an image, a mood, an impression about ourselves in some past action, or thinking about the future will come to mind. Recalling a random thought, image, or impression and writing it down can revive or recall another, jump-starting a train of thinking that can lead to reconstructing a dream.

I've often awakened in the morning and been surprised by the number of dreams I wrote down during the night with no memory of even writing them. At other times, when I only recall a brief scene, I've discovered that writing it down carefully may help the entire dream return to memory. A short time ago I remembered the image of a brown bear from a dream. As I was writing a detailed description of the bear, the dream story began returning and eventually covered three pages.

And now we come to the third important aspect of paying attention to a dream, which is to write it down with all the detail you can. Writing it down carefully helps you to see or feel the full development of the dream. And describing the moods, people, animals, landscapes, and actions in lively ways helps you re-imagine the dream as a story that you can experience again.

In his delightful and wise book *The Star Thrower*, anthropologist Loren Eisley shares a dream in a manner that pulls us directly into it:

> *The dream was of a great blurred bearlike shape emerging from the snow against the window. It pounded on the glass and beckoned importunately toward the forest. I caught the urgency of a message as uncouth and indecipherable as the shape of its huge bearer in the snow. In the immense terror of my dream I struggled against the import of that message as I struggled also to resist the impatient pounding of the frost-enveloped beast at the window.*

Suddenly I lifted the telephone beside my bed, and through the receiver came a message as cryptic as the message from the snow, but far more miraculous in origin. For I knew intuitively, in the still snowfall of my dream, that the voice I heard, a long way off, was my own voice in childhood. Pure and sweet, incredibly refined and beautiful beyond the things of earth, yet somehow inexorable and not to be stayed, the voice was already terminating its messages. "I am sorry to have troubled you," the clear faint syllables of the child persisted. They seemed to come across a thinning wire that lengthened far away into the years of my past. "I am sorry, I am sorry to have troubled you at all." The voice faded before I could speak. I was awake now, trembling in the cold.

As I read this dream I feel like I do when I read a good poem—left with a sense of wonder. Most of us have to relearn how to express ourselves in such a complete manner.

Julia Cameron, in *The Right to Write*, offers useful advice in this direction by urging us to become what she calls "bad writers." By this phrase she means letting everything be expressed even if we think we're describing feelings and events in tabloid terms, where beauties are breathtaking, villains hideous, victims helpless, and murders grizzly. We've been so schooled to censor our feelings, especially in writing, we tend to automatically censor ourselves, putting down "just the facts." When we do this we can end up losing the poetry and flavor of our dreams, like someone who stops digging in a hollow tree a few inches before reaching the honey.

Listening

Listening to the dream includes writing it down as completely as we remember it and including its colorful aspects. However, we must keep in mind that listening to a dream is similar to what we do when we really want someone to listen to us: We want them to put their agendas, their censoring mind-sets, and their "plans" to answer us aside. This is why I like to tell people that while writing the dream down, they should suspend the temptation to interpret it. Likewise, if we're thinking of dream theories and interpretations or problems in our lives, we can't be fully listening to the dream and we're in danger of forcing it into a framework we already have in mind. I once heard someone say that we don't need to kill the bird in order to study it, it's much better to let it sing; and the same is true with dreams.

A second aspect of listening to dreams is also made possible by writing them down—sooner or later we'll have collections of them we can review as dream series. These series are like ongoing conversations with our unconscious, the structure that supports our lives. At one point Jack reviewed his dreams over a period of several months. He first read over them to get a feeling of their different emotional contents. Then he made a list of the main characters and their positive and negative attributes, a list of the places where the dreams took place, and a summary of their story lines and outcomes. He discovered that many of the dreams seemed to fit in the series like chapters in a larger story and his feelings in them appeared like nuances of color in a large painting. This activity can be fun as well as offering important insights into how we're growing and changing, and how some of our dearly held attitudes and beliefs are being consigned to the past.

Questioning

The questions we ask ourselves about our dreams can fall into as many areas as we can imagine. Just as examining a painting reveals its details and beauty, questioning a dream opens up the view of specific scenarios and leaves us wondering where is this place, who are these people, what are they like, why do they keep appearing? We may ask ourselves why this animal, this landscape, this concern, or this dream is appearing in our lives at this particular moment. The unconscious is trying to tell us where our energy is, and where it's going, in the plot or story line of the dream. With this in mind, how the dream is developing and concluding.

Reflecting

Reflecting on our dreams can be like selecting new clothes. We have to try them on and if they seem to fit, we take them. Then we have to wear them for a while and move around in them until they feel comfortable. Similarly, we may mull over a dream's images and moods and consider the questions we've asked and the answers that come to mind as we're trying to figure out how the dream "fits." Finally the dream's components may become part of our lives and change our habitual way of seeing things, especially ourselves. In other words each little bit of new understanding we gain is something we integrate in a manner that expands our awareness.

◆ ◆ ◆

Dreams are the voices within us that offer healing and guidance for our lives. As we saw when Beth met herself in her dream, our dreams connect us to the spirit and source of life within us. They are one of the primary paths to our inner world. Each of our dreams speaks the language of symbols, poetry, and feelings. They are like roots that reach far down into the nourishing earth of our souls and bring the life force up into our growth and healing. They are rooted in our collective unconscious that contains the wisdom of the past and the energy for the future.

Every dream is a personal experience that offers knowledge about ourselves and how we are living, and dreams have the purpose of enlarging our personalities, increasing the scope of our lives, and putting us in touch with the purpose of individuation awakening within us. They show us where we should focus our energy, and they challenge our most tightly drawn defenses as well as our most cherished self-images. They are healing because they bring transformation, energy, and revitalization to portions of us that have been lost or cut off. I'm sorry that I don't have more time to illustrate how to work with them, but you can find help in my book *Sacred Selfishness*.

The art of living is based on our creative response to our unconscious. It is unfortunate, but we find that most people want a good life, good health, and peace of mind, and they also want to keep their lifestyle and their habits and do not want to have to confront themselves and look deeply into their shadows, complexes, and all of the things that Beth's dream told her about.

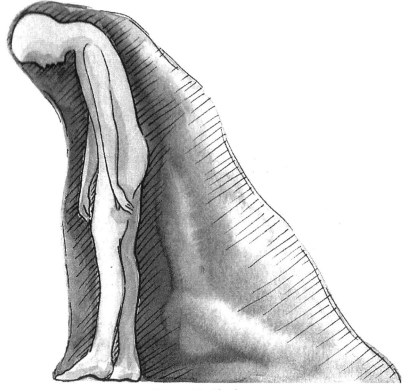

Figure 28. Shadow

But the wealth within us wants to be found, and it tries to reach us through our symptoms, struggles, dreams, and fantasies. But there is a price we will have to pay if we want to tap into the creative and healing potentials within us.

Figure 29. Woman Stepping out of Cage

First, we must learn to value ourselves and our lives enough to step out of our old cages, and value ourselves and our lives enough to see this work as sacred and life-giving, even when it is challenging us to our core. We must devote time, commitment, and study to it as a sacred activity and not regard it as another task to crowd into an overbusy day. We must give it our best energy, not our worn-out, leftover energy. And we must not make the mistake that so many of our religious institutions have made by making these into dogmatic practices that we "inflict" upon ourselves and push ourselves to follow automatically. This approach to valuing our lives as sacred is worth our attention, which means that our love and attention will begin to open doors to our healing and that new passion and creativity will emerge.

Thoughts and Questions to Ponder...

Dreams are the voices within us that offer healing and guidance for our lives. Our dreams connect us to the spirit and source of life within us.

They are one of the primary paths to our inner world.

Begin your dream journal if you haven't already...

List some of the issues you would like to explore in dream time.

Each of our dreams speaks the language of symbols, poetry, and feelings.

Dreams are like roots that reach far down into the nourishing earth of our souls and bring the life force up into our growth and healing. They are rooted in our collective unconscious that contains the wisdom of the past and the energy for the future. Can you remember a dream you have had that taps into this wisdom?

Dreams are important friends and allies for your journey.

Befriending your dreams may provide direction, comfort, and companionship, and sometimes may provide needed confrontation when you are not paying careful attention to your life.

Have you had any dream experiences of this kind?

Instead of trying to "figure out" what the dream is trying to communicate, just be patient and listen as you would to a trusted friend.

Establish an attitude of valuing your dreams, and pay attention by writing them down as soon as you wake up. Write as much detail as you can.

Write down any dreams you have had recently.

Ask questions about your dreams.

What is the meaning of this scene or character for my life at this time? What characteristics of mine could these characters be picturing? Remember, it's your dream. What is your dream communicating to you?

Reflect on your dreams. Allow them to simmer within, mull them over, let them linger in your mind throughout the day as they become part of your life.

How do you think valuing your dreams can increase your feelings of being centered and a whole person?

Be willing to ask if your dream may be showing you about an aspect of yourself that you do not want to see.

Other thoughts...

CHAPTER 23

Journaling to Understanding

And so may a slow
Wind work these words
Of love around you,
An invisible cloak
To mind your life.

— JOHN O'DONOHUE

Journaling is one of our key paths to knowing ourselves and creating a stronger relationship with our lives. Keeping a journal strengthens our personality and helps us objectify our inner life so that we can relate to it better as an "I" and a "Thou." Then we can promote a relationship to it, stimulate our creativity as well as our entire engagement with life.

Through our journals we can amplify our daily experiences and our emotions around them, such as how I felt, how much I felt, and what I really thought. Or we can ask questions like, "Was I diminished?" and "Where is my deepest Self showing up?" Through our journaling we learn that we can only be fully engaged in life through our feelings, yet they can also possess us, become an obsession, or be very painful. Our best course is to objectify them by relating to them concretely, expressing them in our journals, and through dialoging with them, painting them, dancing them, sculpting them. Then we can learn from them, transform them, and contain them, or have them inspire us. I journal about these things in four different ways that include active imagination or dialoging.

When I first suggested journaling to Beth, I asked her to simply write down what seemed like her significant thoughts, feelings, and memories as they occurred during her day. I shared with her that I often journaled in the morning so I could include my dreams and then in the evening to bring my day to a sense of completion. Here are some selections about journaling from my book *Sacred Selfishness: A Guide to Living a Life of Substance* (pp. 154-160) to help you feel comfortable with the process:

Journaling Suggestions

Important Elements in Personal Journal Writing

- Privacy insures trust and provides a space where we can encounter our many aspects truthfully.

- Self-understanding comes from writing down honestly who we are today within the context of our lives.

- Our journals become concrete records over time; studying them can reveal psychological patterns in our lives.

- Examining relationships, feelings, and interactions can be a source for discovering features of ourselves we have denied.

- Including our reflections in our personal journals leads to self-confrontation and to a new consciousness.

In our journals we should include our dreams and our thoughts and responses to them. As we're recording our reflections on the events we've journaled, we can include any new insights, feelings, and other ideas or material that come to mind. It's also a good place to give thought to the feelings and behaviors we had during the day, or to the feelings we didn't get a chance to express. Writing down a description of each situation where we think we feel a particular emotion can often help us get a better understanding of what's happening. For example, one man I know felt resentment whenever his wife suggested he might need a coat, a hat, an umbrella, or something else when he left the house. He thought she was treating him like a child. As he journaled about these situations, he became aware that she might be expressing her care for him, and he was "hearing her like a child" whose mother was chiding him. With this insight he was then able to accept and appreciate her love for him. Journal keeping is both a personal workbook and an intensely personal form of self-expression. Like self-expression itself, there's no right or wrong format. All that matters is that you find a format that works for you, that fits your personality, and that can grow and change with you. Some people I know use elegant notebooks, while others use a computer. I've always been the most comfortable with the kind of spiral notebooks I used in college.

Normal journaling takes about ten or fifteen minutes a day, unless you're exploring something intensely. Then you may take longer, but rarely will you write for more than thirty minutes. People often ask me how they should handle dreams, and I advise them to write the dreams down immediately, whether it's during the night or first thing in the morning. Spouses, lovers, and other people in your home often have to learn to gracefully allow you some time with yourself before you start the day. In many circumstances, keeping dreams attracts interest, and the other people around you might start paying more attention to their own.

Journaling is a particularly good way of reflecting at the end of the day, and many people do it before going to sleep. The time of day or the length of time you devote to journaling, however, can be worked out to fit your own pattern as long as you treat the practice with respect rather than as something you try to conveniently force into your schedule. You may take days off here and there to keep your journaling fresh and from becoming routine and mechanical. Your inner work has its own inner substance—this is the beginning, where you look for it, where you launch the journey deep within yourself.

Tips for Journal Writing

- **Record what is going on or what has happened inside of you as well as outside.**

- **Make special note of strong emotional reactions during the day.**

- **Reflect on these reactions and on the situations and relationships in which they occurred.**

- **Record thoughts, ideas, fantasies, and dreams.**

- **Try to simply reflect on dreams and see what they bring to mind.**

- Record events that surround dreams, and see if they seem related to you.
- Record drawings, poetry, quotations, and whatever else comes to mind.
- Record your personal fantasies and ambitions for both the present and the future.

In the foreword of her lovely and inspiring book *Gift from the Sea*, Anne Morrow Lindbergh explains how the book began as a journal "in order to think out my own particular pattern of living, my own individual balance of life, work and human relationships." She discovered through her writing, and through talking about her writing with other people, that once she looked beneath the surface of life, many men and women in various circumstances and in many forms were "grappling with essentially the same questions."

We are all seeking the sense of security that arrives when we have learned to become more intimate with ourselves. Journaling helps us find assurance that the creativity, values, and ideals that arise inside of us are gifts we can nurture and develop. And when we have found out how to listen to ourselves, we are able to act with strength, greet the world with joy, and share our gifts with others.

Journaling, for most of us, begins with the simple method of recording daily events and the feelings they evoke in us. As we become more at home in this practice, it usually grows into musing, reflection, and self-examination—into seeking to know ourselves more completely. When we help it, the practice of journaling matures, and we discover things about ourselves that we often knew at some level but were unable to formulate or consciously articulate.

Our journals need to be safe places for us to explore spontaneous feelings, thoughts that are still developing, musings, fantasies, and reflections. We grow best when we feel safe—where we're free to express, experiment, and discover who we are in an atmosphere of safety that's grounded in the secure principles of love and self-respect.

Keeping a journal strengthens our personality and helps us objectify our inner life so that we can relate to it better as an "I" and a

"Thou." We can promote a relationship to it as well as stimulate our creativity and our engagement with life.

Here is what I suggest as five ways to journal:
First. I may write down everything that comes to mind, no matter how irrational, with no censorship. This clears the sludge out of my psyche and distances me from my feelings because they are now out from my mind and concretely expressed on paper. The procedure allows me to get a more objective perspective on what I'm feeling and better insight into where it is coming from. Of course, I don't share this with anyone except my analyst. And it is not fair dumping this on a friend or partner, which is really just trying to pass this on to them. For real transformation, we need to hold the tension in our own process.

Second. As in my Darkness Journal, I record the depths of my despair, suffering, fear, grief, anger, loss, and betrayal. It is also the place where I express my envy, my jealousy, and most of all my resentments and the bitter failures of my expectations. The depth of my most human feelings needs a temple that knows them, for in the long run, they teach me the most, as the ancient poet Aeschylus tells us when he says that wisdom emerges drop by drop from the tears of our suffering.

Third. The way I journal is to record my daily experiences, amplify them, and question them. I note strong emotional reactions, and I reflect on relationships and the situations where those strong emotions occurred. I also include fantasies, ambitions, and insights, as well as my dreams.

Fourth. Ultimately, journaling helps us amplify and pull together the narrative of our lives until we touch the deeper flow of the myths we are living that can also support us.

Fifth. I include my active imagination and dialog important inner conversations.

Here are some journal writing suggestions:

1. Allow ten to fifteen minutes a day to record inner and outer happenings.

2. Note strong emotional reactions, and reflect on the relationships and situations in which they occurred.

3. Record fantasies, ambitions, ideas, and insights.

4. Record dreams and your reflections on dreams.

5. Contents must be considered private and should not be shared.

6. A journal is a safe place to explore, reflect, express, and discover who you are.

7. Remember, there is no right or wrong way to express yourself.

Allow yourself to be creative in selecting just the right journal, perhaps a special leather-bound one, or make your own special cover. And allow yourself to be creative in how and what you write in your journal. One woman's journal contained letters to God written during cancer treatment. She gave herself permission to be angry with God at times, to express her dark, confused thoughts and feelings, and to express her gratitude. Her journal became a place of complete honesty with herself and the Divine.

Active Imagination

Active imagination now covers a wide range of activities in Jungian psychology. The basic purpose of it is to use our imaginations as active fields where we can intentionally discover and come into relationship with aspects of ourselves we don't understand and know little about. Active imagination gives both form and voice to these elements of our personalities that normally aren't heard, and it establishes lines of communication with them. It can take place through drawing, painting, writing, sculpting, dancing, and making music.

Creating objective inner relationships by actively using imagination enables you to intentionally discover and come into relationship with aspects of yourself you don't understand or know little about. Active imagination can give voice to parts of you in need of being recognized and heard. Dialoging, as I have illustrated, is an especially effective means of listening to and learning from inner parts of yourself like anger, fear, the inner critic, depression, symptoms, illnesses, feelings, body parts, dream figures, and fantasy figures. Dialoging is a way of making the unconscious known.

You have several examples of active imagination or dialoging to guide you: Beth's dream figure and my dialog with cancer. Remember, active imagination is about meeting the image for what it is and entering into dialog with it so that something can happen.

Example: If reading this material is giving you a headache, dialog with it.

You: Head, why are you aching when you read this material?

Head: Because I'm on overload. Besides, the heart has the answers…

The dialog has begun, just go with it.

You may wonder how it is possible to dialog with parts of "yourself"…At first, you may feel silly or uncomfortable. If you think you are making it up, don't become discouraged. Stay with the process that is coming from within you. After a time or two, dialoging will be a natural process to which you will look forward. There is a release of energy that enables you to live with clarity and a depth of awareness and self-knowing; awkwardness is replaced with energy. By all means, write out your dialogs, either by hand or on the computer. By actually putting your feelings and thoughts in writing, it takes them from the abstract and makes them concrete.

Thoughts and Questions to Ponder...

Suggestions for Dialoging:

How to begin to dialog with parts of "yourself":

Create a special, private place. Turn off your cell phone or other phone.

Start by writing your name and asking a question of some part of yourself.

Wait, breathe, and trust that the words you hear in your mind in response are true and accurate.

Write these words down.

Respond by writing whatever occurs to you, just as in a dialog with someone in the outer world.

Now that you have the rhythm and form, just continue listening, responding, and writing.

Pay close attention to your energy, how you feel at the beginning and at the end.

Remember this is sacred work. Breathe, take your time. Trust in the power of your inner world.

Take an extended amount of time to dialog with parts of yourself... your hidden parts...and journal this dialog.

Explore how this kind of journaling can help you think about your own particular pattern of living, your own "individual balance of life, work, and human relationships." What you have been discovering about yourself?

Take time one day this week to journal and record what is going on or what has happened inside of you as well as outside.

As you journal, make special note of strong emotional reactions during the day. Reflect on these reactions and on the situations and relationships in which they occurred.

Other thoughts...

CHAPTER 24

Rituals as Stepping Stones

May you travel in an awakened way,
Gathered wisely into your inner ground;
That you may not waste the invitations
Which wait along the way to transform you.

– JOHN O'DONOHUE

The final creative path to the unconscious that I want to talk about is that of rituals. Rituals facilitate our transition from one state of mind to another one. They help us to separate and sever our links and attachments to parts of our old selves. They also help us reconcile the reality of the changes we are experiencing, especially brutal ones such as maturing, loss, and death. They can also be a way of being in touch in with the sacred, the Self, and with new potentials.

Developing rituals can carry us through losses, depression, despair, and difficult passages. They can help us honor our suffering, fear, grief, anger, loss, and betrayal. This then helps make all our other practices and treatments more effective.

When Gail was going through her chemotherapy for her breast cancer, she and her husband made a ritual of gathering her hair that fell out in the shower and burying it in the nearby woods. This ritual was honoring the old and preparing for the new, as well as honoring her sadness and hope.

When I returned home from my surgery, I helped myself relax in order to sleep by creating a ritual of imagery. I chose to imagine myself as the prodigal son being welcomed home by his father in Rembrandt's famous painting. For this to be effective, I had to place myself in the scene as the son. I had to be present and hear my father's voice as he said, "Welcome home," to feel his hand upon my shoulder, and his embrace. I did this for about two weeks, and it helped calm me at night and reassured me that a new life, a change of fate, was possible.

In another case, I knew that my prostate was the first vital part of me to go from dust to dust, and I wondered how to honor and ritualize its passing. Should I give it a symbolic funeral, a memorial service, or some kind of celebration? Nothing seemed to click. Then I thought of the Jewish Kaddish, a service recited each day at the beginning of the day of burial and lasting daily for eleven months. This devotion is intended as an act of reverence and praise of God. The idea, not the actual form, resonated with me, and I wrote a prayer of reverence and thankfulness for my prostate which I recited daily for several weeks.

Figure 30. Rembrandt's painting

So this has been a brief discussion of examples of these creative paths into the roots of our deeper selves. Of course, we have only touched the surface, but I wonder if in general you can see their value, and if you can take a few minutes to write about some of the rituals in your life—or if you don't have any, ask yourself, "Why not?"

Rituals

1. Take sacred time.
2. Rituals are to be loved and desired, not inflicted.
3. Make use of sacred symbols
4. Purpose: to bring peace, comfort, hope, and inner connectedness as vehicles of transitions and transformation

Example of a simple ritual:

As I light this candle and see the smoke rising,

I remember the value of my prostate in the quality of my life and in my living future, pictured by my children and by my manhood reflected in the mirror. It has gone from my body to begin a journey that I am not ready to take.

Its departure reminds me of the purpose and vitality that I still have to commit to the journey of life.

I will leave this candle and this table in celebration of my life and its growing journey.

Thoughts and Questions to Ponder...

Now is the time to think about and design your own ritual.

Allow your imagination to guide you.

Your ritual can be very simple or expanded.

Start by taking some deep breaths while sitting in silence.

Then begin...

In your ritual, consider taking to heart the Grail questions that we have been working with...

It is important to return to these questions again and again in the next days and months and to be with these questions, to live them, to ponder them, and to be willing to trust the answers that come to you.

Ask yourself with compassion...at your soul level:

What ails thee?

What is troubling you at a core level?

...In silence, breathe deeply for a few minutes.

Whom does the Grail serve?

...Remember, we come to learn that the Grail—the source of life—is there to help us.

...And how can I help?

...and that we ourselves can, in turn, serve the Grail—the source of life...

Openness, trust, and patience are required to ask these questions.

Other thoughts...

CHAPTER 25

Conclusion: The Light in the Dark

May you learn to receive it graciously,
And promise to learn swiftly
That it may leave you newborn,
Willing to dedicate your time to birth.

— JOHN O'DONOHUE

When I originally wrote "Radical Hope: A Guide to the Healing Power of Illness" for a lecture and seminar scheduled in 2012, I didn't realize it would transform into this book. I actually ended up canceling that lecture after it had been fully publicized and less than a week before I was to give it. Somewhere deep inside of me, a voice was telling me I couldn't do it. Something was wrong. I had missed something. I had failed to face and understand something. As days turned into months, I struggled with my reflections about it.

I knew that my cancer had changed and transformed my life. The power of this transformation surprised me because my life had been devoted to growth and transformation. Through my practice, I had spent decades helping people heal, grow, and realize potentials within themselves beyond what they could have imagined. I also knew that as dramatically as my cancer had affected me, I am one of the lucky ones. Many people, including ones I had been and am working with, had it far worse than I did. My reflections took me back in my history, deep into the feelings I had as a small boy while my mother was dying of cancer. I was too young to understand that the only way our suffering can find meaning is through personal transformation. My mother was forced to choose between making her journey a spiritual quest or yielding to desolation. As we watched her flesh waste away, we also witnessed the power of her spiritual transformation. But I, as a boy, had a heart filled with grief, loss, and rage—powerful emotions that stunned me so deeply that it took me over twenty years and plenty of analysis to emerge into a full life again.

As my reflections continued about this theme, I began to wonder if her illness was the gateway to her individuation, the key to opening her life to her wholeness and destiny. Was her illness the path that was in the pattern of her life that was meant to influence her entire community? I also asked myself, "Was her destiny and the way it crushed me, and over time moved me, some of the birth pains of my own destiny?" I wrote in chapter 17 about the horror and the beauty of life—that an illness could be one's journey into wholeness, one's individuation. That one's destiny was a horror/beauty was a concept that I had a great deal of resistance to even thinking about.

The conflict I felt as I considered the possibility of this horror/beauty dynamic was compounded by my daughter's progressive multiple sclerosis. I searched into the psychology of illness as I never had before. For years I had known the difference between simply being healed and being transformed into a person of awe who inspired others, but I didn't want this journey for my daughter. I wanted her to be cured, to be pain free, to be free of fear and suffering. I wanted her to have a healthy life full of peace and laughter.

Even as I write these words, I remember other people who were inspiring to me. Laurie Masterson comes to mind as an inspiration to our entire community. She owned a popular restaurant and struggled with what I understood to be a genetic form of continually recurring cancer. Laurie was also an inspiring athlete in the midst of her suffering. For over two decades, she inspired us by spreading her bumper sticker, "Don't Postpone Joy," throughout our city.

But I didn't want my daughter to become inspiring. I wanted her to be cured. I hoped beyond hope that somewhere in my professional expertise, I could find a way to help this cure take place. I had to face the fact that I couldn't, and that without realizing it, I had focused my work on my 2012 lecture and seminar in that direction and that hope. I was right to cancel it, because I was failing to realize that whatever we want to call it, the big Self, destiny, the Divine or whatever…something bigger and more mysterious than I could accept was working and being lived in our lives. I was far more defended against the horror and the beauty of life than I had thought I was. This armor also cut me off from the mystery and depth in the human spirit which I can now think of only as Divine.

Marjorie has gone on to become an inspiring person in her world as her body grinds down. She created "Team Marge at Large," a fundraising event that has raised a lot of money for the National MS Society. She has also become a teacher and a speaker, and she leads an interdenominational Bible study group. Her family supports her lovingly and does its best to keep her active and involved—as you see her son and husband on a hike here in the mountains.

Figure 31. Marjorie at a rally. *Figure 32. Marjorie on a hike with her husband and son.*

The horror and the beauty—I cannot help being filled with sadness, love, and awe. My reflections carried me forward to the other inspiring people I've mentioned in this book. Tom Swift, lying helpless, found a way to share the depth of his spirit and experience with us—the depth of the human spirit and experience. Viktor Frankl emerged from hell to help countless thousands of people, and his writings also helped bring me to life. Carl Jung's great life work that is beyond measure emerged from his dark night of the soul.

Beth and others like her that I have had the honor to work with, actually the honor to be part of their lives, have been inspirations as well.

In these circumstances, I have been able to witness the life force emanating through their unconscious from their greater Self, their center. With a little recognition from us, this force comes forth…seeking purpose, meaning, and a life being healed. It seems as if this force is awakened by our circumstances, but it is not due to them. It is due to our response to them—our choosing to seek a new horizon. On this path, our lives are not an image of failure, defeat, and deterioration. They become a landscape that, when its depth is entered into, becomes one of hope, love, and meaning, ushering in a new range of possibilities.

A final urge to accept this horror/beauty came from a very special DVD. The title is *The Appointment with the Wise Old Dog: Dream Images in a Time of Crisis*. This documentary shows the experiences of David Blum in his journey with cancer. Here is a brief description from the film's Facebook page: "David was an internationally known orchestra conductor and author. Diagnosed with cancer at the age of 52, he discovered that drawing images from his dreams helped him cope with his illness in a profoundly unexpected way. Blum gently leads the viewer into his drawings reflecting spiritual guides, including his beloved deceased dachshund; radiant landscapes; and the music of Mozart and Beethoven. Shortly before his death, Blum felt compelled to share his inner journey in the hope that his personal experience could help others realize their own inner gifts. In this moving documentary, Blum explains: 'It's an amazing fact that at a time of dire crisis, people often unexpectedly find themselves supported by a power that makes it possible for them to cope.'" David not only supported my ability to cope. He also showed the power and love from the deeper Self that can support our lives.

I have seen some of the people I've worked with bring their illness to a standstill. In the early 1990s, I worked with Dick, who brought his AIDS to a standstill through this work and through his medical treatment. The Jungian analyst Guy Corneau, whom I have mentioned frequently in this book, brought his stage IV cancer to a standstill by seeking the best medical treatment, the best alternative care, and by stopping his life and devoting all his energy to his healing, inner journey, active imagination, and transformation.

I could fill another book with inspiring stories. But my intention is not just to inspire you. It is to give you a map of the journey and support for bringing your own inspiring journey to life. So this book outlines a journey of healing and of leaving the shell of our old life behind. This journey can surely bring healing, and it may bring a cure or it may not. But the journey is worth it, for it puts us in touch with the life force, the core of ourselves, and what I can only call the Divine.

In chapter 7, I shared the section on "The Measure of the Human Spirit" with you. As I bring this book to a close, I want to repeat a portion of this section because I think it is so important for our journey…through illness and through life. As we travel through life, our responses to pain and death are often the greatest measures of how precious we know life to be, and they are also a measure of the human spirit because we make them a measure of our spirit.

The Measure of the Human Spirit

All too often we think of heroism as winning, conquering, defeating, overcoming all odds, and having a positive attitude. And as we pursue this course, we invariably fall into our subtle addiction to perfection, even in our spiritual pursuits. But when midlife, aging, trauma, or illness throw us into the search for meaning that activates a radical shift in life, we need to find the support of our own depths and the Divine within us—the Self with a capital S. This journey back into our full humanity calls for a new kind of heroism. This heroism is to face our fate and say yes to it…to what is already happening to us…to dive into it and into own our depths.

This is the turn that Parsifal made when he turned from being a glorious knight of King Arthur's Round Table, the fulfillment of a child-hood dream, into a knight seeking the Holy Grail. Parsifal was willing to ask the right questions of the Grail in order to bring new life and whole-ness into the wasteland—the symbol of our inner state. It is the turn that Chiron the centaur made in Greek mythology when he gave up eternal life and the inflated sense that he could be his own redeemer. After that, Chiron chose to cooperate with the forces that shaped him and at that moment was transformed from a tragic victim into a courageous seeker, one who was prepared to plunge into the unknown search for healing, wholeness, authenticity, and a new dynamic spirit of life. By doing this, he became the guiding archetypal spirit of the wounded healer. When we are in pain—whether it is psychological, emotional, or physical—by making this turn toward the hero or heroine's quest, this choice lessens the pain. This is a key component of the healing process.

Drinking from the chalice of destiny means facing my fate and calling on my deeper Self for love and support. Doing this lifts me out of the victimhood of an unconscious fate and sets me on the classic hero's quest that Dr. Carl Jung and the mythologist Joseph Campbell spoke so much about. It gives radical rebirth—transformation—to anyone who chooses this path, and it gives them the possibility of helping to renew and transform our culture.

This whole journey that I am presenting is directed toward us finding meaning and individuation through our illnesses. It is choosing the path of being a seeker. It is a radical perspective that brings radical hope as we learn to understand that individuation itself is a radical series of transformations. As we realize that initiation is the rite of dying to an old life and being born into a new one, we see that illness, as an initiation, initiates us continually into knowing what it means to become more fully human. And becoming more fully human initiates us into becoming truly spiritual.

The classic hero or heroine's quest always results in bringing new values back to the culture. So the next question is,

"How can we bring new values from our illness to our culture?"

Again, let me tell you how we can do it...

If we live our illness with support from our Self or depths and do it humbly.

If we become open to carrying our suffering and fear openly but with grace, after accepting the full presence of them.

If we become open to letting others fully express their caring for us, and if we are willing to be trouble in their lives.

If we are willing to be seen in our vulnerability and humiliations.

If we stand unashamedly for life until we know deep inside that it is time for us to accept our death.

What I am saying is that if we can open ourselves to receive love, care, and compassion, and be willing to be dependent on others, we offer them the gift of discovering their best capacities as human beings. Then we become significant participants in the redemption of our culture. Then we are helping to loosen the stranglehold our culture has on us that calls us to always be positive, productive, busy, and self-critical.

Now we can help our culture learn what it means to be truly human—to place compassion above productivity and community above individualism...and to place love above busyness...and to learn that our quest for the Divine is a quest to become fully human. Then we have come to understand why all of our great religions so conspicuously value suffering, and we can see that our suffering, our illness, has a meaning and a profound role to play in teaching our world how to cherish the greatest values life has to offer.

This has been a heartbreakingly difficult journey for me. Yet it has also brought great moments of love and joy. And the journey continues. I hope that what I am learning and sharing will also make your own life richer and more hopeful.

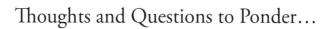

Thoughts and Questions to Ponder...

This journey to a place beyond normal...where radical hope lives and flourishes on a daily basis...has become the most important journey that you can take.

Reflect on how this journey can be an ongoing daily practice for yourself.

This map of the journey is here to support you for bringing your own inspiring journey to life...a journey of healing and of leaving the shell of your old life behind.

"Accepting the darkness is a radical change in our perspective, and deepening it is even more radical." There is value in accepting the dark spaces within us and in experiencing the full reality of our fear, pain, and loss.

Have you come to understand...and to accept your own dark caverns...more?

Have you come to move beyond fear, anxiety, and reluctance... to breathe into those deep aspects of yourself...and to listen to the wisdom of your wounds?

This journey can bring healing—it may bring a cure or it may not—but the journey itself is worth it, for it puts us in touch with the life force, the core of ourselves, the Divine. Beginning to recognize and actively notice this life force within us activates its coming forth and bringing purpose, meaning, and a healing.

What are your reflections?

Someone once wrote that every moment receives a blessing from the heart of the world...do you have a sense deep inside of how that is possible...for you on your journey?

In mapping this journey, we have seen illness as an initiation that initiates us into knowing what it means to become more fully human...and that becoming more fully human initiates us into becoming truly spiritual when we choose the path of being a seeker.

What else can you bring to mapping this journey?

Cultivating this kind of deep perspective is a daily practice… of observing and noticing what we seem to habitually "sweep away"…

What are the ways that would support you cultivating this deep perspective and remembering and being in touch with this new aspect of yourself?

Your commitment to yourself to seek self-knowledge, self-love, and self-valuing as a sacred carrier of life brings you the power to live a meaningful life—a life of purpose, balance, and fulfillment.

To encourage this, it is important to continue to dialog with this new aspect of yourself that is emerging…

Other thoughts…

Ongoing Reflections for the Journey

This whole journey is directed toward us finding meaning and individuation through our illnesses. It is choosing the path of being a seeker. It is a radical perspective that brings radical hope as we learn to understand that individuation itself is a radical series of transformations. As we realize that initiation is the rite of dying to an old life and being born into a new one, we see that illness, as an initiation, initiates us continually into knowing what it means to become more fully human. And becoming more fully human initiates us into becoming truly spiritual.

RESOURCES

Achterberg, Jeanne, Barbara Dossey, and Leslie Kolkmeier. *Rituals of Healing.* New York: Bantam Books, 1994.

Blum, David. *Appointment with the Wise Old Dog: Dream Images in a Time of Crisis.* DVD. 1998.

Bolen, Jean Shinoda. *Close to the Bone: Life-Threatening Illness and the Search for Meaning.* New York: Simon & Schuster, 1996.

Campbell, Joseph. *The Hero with a Thousand Faces.* New Jersey: Princeton University Press, 1973.

———. *Pathways to Bliss.* California: New World Library, 2004.

Corneau, Guy. "To Live Again." Lecture and Workshop. Jung Society of Atlanta. Sept. 18, 2015.

Cousins, Norman. *Anatomy of an Illness as Perceived by the Patient: Reflections on Healing and Regeneration.* New York: W.W. Norton & Company, Inc., 1979.

———. *Head First: The Biology of Hope and the Healing Power of the Human Spirit.* New York: Penguin Books, 1990.

Duff, Kat. *The Alchemy of Illness.* New York: Bell Tower, 1993.

Frankl, Viktor E. *The Unheard Cry for Meaning: Psychotherapy and Humanism.* New York: Simon & Schuster, 1978.

———. *Man's Search for Meaning.* New York: Simon & Schuster, 1984.

———. *The Will to Meaning: Foundations and Applications of Logotherapy.* New York: New American Library, Inc., 1970.

Gordon, Rosemary. *Dying and Creating: A Search for Meaning.* London: H. Karnac Books Ltd., 2000.

Harris, Bud, and Massimilla Harris. *Like Gold Through Fire: Understanding the Transforming Power of Suffering.* California: Fisher King Press, 1996.

Harris, Bud. *Knowing the QUESTIONS, Living the ANSWERS: A Jungian Guide Through the Paradoxes of Peace, Conflict, and Love that Mark a Lifetime.* South Carolina: CreateSpace, 2010.

———. *Sacred Selfishness: A Guide to Living a Life of Substance.* Hawaii: Inner Ocean Publishing, 2002.

Hillman, James. *The Dream and the Underworld.* Harper and Row, 1979.

Lipton, Bruce H. *The Biology of Belief: Unleashing the Power of Consciousness, Matter and Miracles.* Hay House, 2008.

Jung, C. G. *Nietzsche's Zarathustra: Notes of the Seminar Given 1934–1939.* Ed. James L. Jarrett. New Jersey: Princeton University Press, 1988.

————. *Alchemical Studies*. Trans. R.F.C. Hull. Volume 13 of Collected Works. New Jersey: Princeton University, 1983.

Kast, Verena. *Imagination as Space of Freedom: Dialogue between the Ego and the Unconscious*. Trans. Anselm Hollo. New York: Fromm International Publishing Corporation, 1993.

————. *Joy, Inspiration, and Hope*. Trans. Douglas Whitcher. New York: Fromm International Publishing Corporation, 1994.

Kearney, Michael. *Mortally Wounded: Stories of Soul Pain, Death, and Healing*. Louisiana: Spring Journal, 2007.

————. *A Place of Healing: Working with Nature & Souls and the End of Life*. Louisiana: Spring Journal, 2009.

Kleinman, Arthur. *The Illness Narratives: Suffering, Healing and the Human Condition*. New York: Basic Books, 1988.

Kreinheder, Albert. *Body and Soul: The Other Side of Illness*. 1991. 2nd Edition. Canada: Inner City Books, 2009.

Lear, Jonathan. *Radical Hope: Ethics in the Face of Cultural Devastation*. Massachusetts: Harvard University Press, 2008.

McGilchrist, Iain. *The Master and his Emissary: The Divided Brain and the Making of the Western World*. Yale University Press, 2009.

McTaggart, Lynne. *The Field: The Quest for the Secret Force of the Universe*. Harper, 2008.

Moyers, Bill. *Healing and the Mind*. Ed. Betty Sue Flowers. New York: Doubleday, 1993.

Nelson, Gertrud Mueller. *To Dance with God: Family Ritual and Community Celebration*. New York: Paulist Press, 1986.

Nepo, Mark. *Inside the Miracle: Enduring Suffering, Approaching Wholeness*. Sounds True, 2015.

Price, Reynolds. *A Whole New Life: An Illness and a Healing*. New York: MacMillan Publishing Company, 1994.

Rossman, Martin L. *Guided Imagery for Self-Healing: An Essential Resource for Anyone Seeking Wellness*. 2nd Edition. California: New World Library, 2000.

Sanford, John A. *Dreams and Healing*. New York: Paulist Press, 1978.

Sacks, Oliver. *Gratitude*. Knopf, 2015.

Sarno, John E. *The Divided Mind: The Epidemic of Mindbody Disorders*. Regan, Harper Collins, 2006.

Spring Vol. 82, Symbolic Life 2009: A Journal of Archetype and Culture. Ed. Nancy Carter. Louisiana: Spring Journal, Fall 2009.

Ulanov, Ann Belford. *Attacked by Poison Ivy: A Psychological Understanding.* Maine: Nicolas-Hays, Inc., 2001.

Wikman, Monika. *Pregnant Darkness: Alchemy and the Rebirth of Consciousness.* Maine: Nicolas-Hays, Inc., 2004.

Woodman, Marion. *Bone: Dying into Life.* New York: The Penguin Group, 2000.

A Note of Thanks

Whether you received *Radical Hope and the Healing Power of Illness* as a gift, borrowed it from a friend, or purchased it yourself, we're glad you read it. We think that Bud Harris is a refreshing, challenging, and inspiring voice, and we hope you will share this book and his thoughts with your family and friends. If you would like to learn more about Bud Harris, Ph.D., and his work, please visit: www.budharris.com or https://www.facebook.com/BudHarrisPh.D.

About the Author

Bud Harris, Ph.D., as a Jungian analyst, writer, and lecturer, has dedicated his life to helping people grow through their challenges and life situations into becoming "the best versions of themselves." Bud originally became a businessman in the corporate world and then owned his own business. Though very successful, he began to search for a new version of himself and life when, at age thirty-five, he became dissatisfied with his accomplishments in business and was challenged by serious illness in his family. At this point, Bud returned to graduate school to become a psychotherapist. After earning his Ph.D. in psychology and practicing as a psychotherapist and psychologist, he experienced the call to further his growth and become a Jungian analyst. He then moved to Zurich, Switzerland, where he trained for over five years and graduated from the C. G. Jung Institute.

Bud is the author of thirteen informative and inspiring books. He writes and teaches with his wife, Jungian analyst Massimilla Harris, Ph.D., and lectures widely. Bud and Massimilla both practice as Jungian analysts in Asheville, North Carolina.

For more information about his practice and work, visit:

www.budharris.com
or
https://www.facebook.com/BudHarrisPh.D.

Printed in Great Britain
by Amazon